SCORING
FOR
PERCUSSION

SCORING

FOR

PERCUSSION

and the Instruments of the Percussion Section

H. Owen Reed

Professor of Music
Michigan State University

Joel T. Leach

Assistant Professor of Music
Texas Technological College

PRENTICE-HALL, INC., Englewood Cliffs, New Jersey

Printed in the United States of America

Library of Congress Catalog Card No.: 69–12824

Current printing (last digit):
10 9 8 7 6 5 4 3 2 1

PRENTICE-HALL INTERNATIONAL, INC., London
PRENTICE-HALL OF AUSTRALIA, PTY. LTD, Sydney
PRENTICE-HALL OF CANADA, LTD., Toronto
PRENTICE-HALL OF INDIA PRIVATE LTD., New Delhi
PRENTICE-HALL OF JAPAN, INC., Tokyo

Table of Contents

3

The Metallic Instruments   45

4

The Wooden Instruments   64

NOTATION AND SCORING

8

The Full Score   117

9

The Percussion Parts   122

10

Percussion as an Integral Part of the Compositional Scheme   128

Introduction

Imagine a small symphony orchestra whose woodwind section is composed of all woodwind specialists. Although the clarinetist is most proficient on the Clarinets, he can also play the Piccolo, Flute, Oboe, English Horn, Bassoon, and Contra Bassoon. This ability to play *all* of the woodwind instruments is evident throughout the section. Imagine, too, that on the score the composer wrote the woodwinds on only three staffs. Although the Flute and Piccolo would primarily occupy the top staff, other woodwind instruments might also be written there. The second and third staffs would likewise serve for the notation of any woodwind instrument. In fact, one of the staffs might, for example, be used for Oboe 1 and English Horn playing simultaneously (stems up and down) and, after a few measures, each would change to Clarinet and Bassoon, respectively.

Imagine, then, that all the music is passed out to the members of the orchestra. (Each woodwind player would have a part—in the form of a woodwind score.) The conductor enters, and the first rehearsal is about to start:

Maestro: All right, orchestra . . . from the beginning.
Woodwind Player: Maestro, if you please, we haven't yet decided how to
    divide up our playing responsibilities.
  M.: Please hurry, then.
W.P.: Yes, Maestro.
  M.: Now may we please begin?
W.P.: Maestro, the music is written so that we must have *two* B-flat Clarinets.
    Since both are sounding at once, we'll have to rush out and get another Clarinet.
  M.: Please hurry!
W.P.: While we are waiting, Maestro, will you please check at measure 19. I
    have to change from English Horn to Bassoon in only two measures!

M.: Two measures is correct. If you can't move the Bassoon closer and make the change, see if you can't get one of the other performers to cover the Bassoon at that spot.

W.P.: I can, if someone else can cover the Piccolo part at measure 25.

M.: Well, try to work it out among yourselves somehow. Now that we have two Clarinets, can we begin?

W.P.: One more minute, Maestro. The composer wrote a low B for the Flute, and my model only goes down to C.

M.: Then play an octave higher. No one will notice it anyway. Now please let's. . . .

W.P.: Maestro! One more question before we get started. The composer calls for a Heckelphone. We don't own a Heckelphone, and the only one I know of is on rental at Maurie's Woodwind Shop in Chicago.

M.: There's neither time nor money for rental. Stuff a sock in the bell of the Contra Bassoon and play it on that. And now. . . .

W.P.: Maestro! I *am* sorry, but do you know if the composer plans for the Piccolo to sound as written or an octave higher? He doesn't say on the part.

M.: Well, it's rather difficult to tell the exact octave of a Piccolo; but no doubt, since he is an American composer, he wants it to sound an octave higher. After all we are *not* in Mozambique! Now if we may. . . .

W.P.: Maestro! This composer must have majored in plumbing! At measure 79 he has written a glissando on the Flute from low C to the G above my highest C. Obviously I can't play that high G except on the Piccolo, and it would be almost impossible to change without a rather noticeable break!

M.: Naturally! Then change the G to an octave lower and play it all on the Flute! And, by the way, why don't you write the composer about this? He would no doubt appreciate it, and you might suggest that he use the traditional note heads. Music is difficult enough to read without using x-headed notes for the double reeds and diamond-headed notes for the single reeds. . . . Now can we *please* start rehearsing? The percussion section is getting restless!

W.P.: Just one more question, Maestro. I specialize on the Flute and Piccolo, but the composer asks me to change to Bassoon for a rather difficult solo at measure 50. Wouldn't it be better if we had another copy of the woodwind score duplicated so that Pierre could play this?

M.: By all means . . . if we ever do play it! And now, Gentlemen, *if we may!*

M.: (*after a few measures of rehearsal*) Now where was the clarinet at measure 20?

W.P.: Maestro, the composer has allowed us so little time to change from one instrument to another that we will need to make a placement chart.

M.: (*screaming*) Manager! Librarian! Please collect the parts and score and return them immediately to the composer. Tell him that because of unforeseen circumstances we will have to postpone the performance of his work until a later date. And now, Gentlemen, please put up *Eine kleine Nachtmusik!*

Rather chaotic, isn't it? This couldn't really happen! No? But it does . . . *in the percussion section!* Time after time!

The above analogy only helps to dramatize a problem badly in need of clarification. Every year composers and arrangers become more aware of the potentials inherent in percussion instruments. But in spite of this, they are timid in using them. This can usually be traced to a lack of information concerning the following:

a) *Availability of the various percussion instruments*

Which instruments are found in professional and school orchestras and bands? Although the composer must at times be practical, the problem of instrument availability should generally be the responsibility of the performers. Most of the instruments discussed in Chapter 1 through Chapter 4 and the first seven in Chapter 5 *should* be available. If not, they can be rented or borrowed, if the composition merits the expense and inconvenience—and if time permits. And if this is impractical, have faith in the percussionist. He is a master at substitution.

b) *Ranges of instruments[1] and sizes available*

Are instrument sizes standardized? Are ranges consistently specified in manufacturers' brochures and in orchestration books? The answer is a definite no! Until recently percussion manufacturers have been reluctant to standardize. The Marimba, for example, can be purchased in several sizes with ranges extending from 2 1/2 octaves to 4 1/4 octaves. A great discrepancy also exists in the recommended ranges for the Timpani.

---

[1]In discussing ranges, the following method for designating the octave will be used:

Middle C

$$AAA\text{-}BBB; \quad CC\text{-}BB; \quad C\text{-}B; \quad c\text{-}b; \quad c^1\text{-}b^1; \quad c^2\text{-}b^2; \quad c^3\text{-}b^3; \quad c^4\text{-}b^4; \quad c^5$$

1st 8ve   2nd 8ve   3rd 8ve   4th 8ve   5th 8ve   6th 8ve   7th 8ve

c) *Transpositions of the Mallet Percussion Instruments*

What are the exact octave transpositions of the Mallet Percussion Instruments? Because of the acoustical peculiarities of certain instruments, there is a lack of agreement concerning the transposition of the Chimes, Orchestra Bells, and Xylophone.

d) *Ways of setting instruments into vibration*

Should there not be more discussion of this subject? Generally, only the most conventional means of setting percussion instruments into vibration have been presented.

e) *Various types of beaters*[2]

Do the composers or arrangers know what choices are available? Or if they do, what sounds the various beaters produce? Yet the composer must have this knowledge to write in a sensitive manner for percussion.

f) *Standardized notation*

Should a single line or a five-line staff be used for percussion notation? Which lines or spaces are used? What clef? What kinds of note heads? There is great need for *some* standardization of percussion notation.

Although each of the traditional orchestration books contains one or more chapters on percussion, obvious discrepancies and some inaccuracies occur. The improvements in percussion instruments, some recent attempts at their standardization, and the popularity of new and imported instruments have created the need for a new look at these problems. *Scoring for Percussion* attempts to do this.

This study of percussion writing is not all-inclusive. Such a work would encompass an infinite number of volumes and include an equally infinite number of percussive sounds. Rather, it is limited to those instruments normally available and in use, with the more obscure instruments and special sound effects grouped together and listed in Chapter 6.

[2]The beaters listed for each instrument include those in general use and available through commercial outlets, although some mallets *not to be used* are also listed. (This is to caution the composer against specifying a mallet which is damaging to the instrument.) Percussionists often make their own mallets from various materials and in varying sizes and shapes. In line with the physical characteristics of beaters, the authors hope to solve a problem of semantics by grouping them as follows:

Mallets: Timpani, Tenor Drum, Bass Drum, Xylophone, Marimba, Vibe, Glockenspiel, and Chime.
Sticks: Snare Drum and Timbale.
Beaters: Triangle. (Also used for general classification.)

Even the sounds produced by commercially available instruments are inexhaustible; but once a composer starts to think creatively in percussion writing and understands how to notate for the percussion instruments—as he does with the other choirs of the orchestra or band—endless possibilities will occur to him.

In order to accumulate practical information about the availability of instruments, ranges, sizes, etc., the authors surveyed the percussion sections of many professional and college orchestras, referred to many orchestration books and percussion methods, and corresponded with numerous percussionists and the manufacturers of percussion instruments. Interestingly, the percussion profession presented many contradictory opinions on such questions as range, transposition, and nomenclature. Contradictions were also evident in information gathered from other sources, but the survey was generally informative. The material in the following chapters attempts to clarify the many confusing and conflicting practices and to standardize some of the elusive practices.

For all this valuable information and advice the authors are grateful, and all contributors are listed in Appendix 2.

The Percussion Instruments

The Mallet
Percussion Instruments   **1**

THE XYLOPHONE

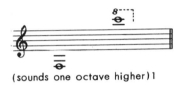

(sounds one octave higher)[1]

The Xylophone is probably the best known of all the mallet percussion instruments. Its keyboard is made of thick wooden bars (usually rosewood) which are tuned specifically to each bar's fundamental and third partial. When struck with hard mallets the bars produce a brittle, glassy tone. The Xylophone may or may not have resonators.

Xylophones are generally manufactured in only two sizes: 3 chromatic octaves, with a written range from c^1 to c^4, and 3 1/2 chromatic octaves, from f to c^4. The larger instrument is the one most commonly used in college and professional organizations.

The Xylophone tone is extremely brilliant and well-defined, but of short duration—about two seconds at forte level. Recording experts have remarked that the Xylophone's tone reproduces with better fidelity than that of any other musical instrument. The tone quality can be somewhat altered by the choice of beaters.

[1]All ranges shown are written ranges. In each instance the whole note represents the conservative range which can be assumed to embrace all but the smallest and least expensive instruments. The filled-in note heads represent the extreme range of the larger instruments or the range possible under ideal circumstances.

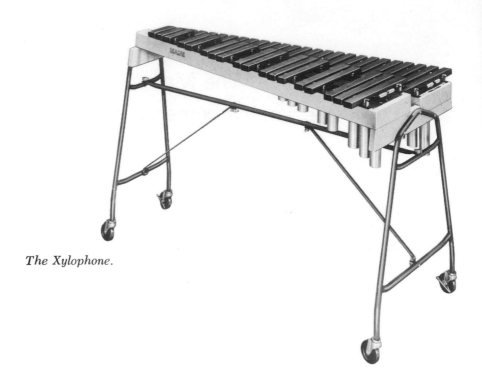

The Xylophone.

BEATERS

Brass mallets—not to be used; will damage bars of Xylophone.

Plastic mallets—typical Xylophone sound.

Wood mallets—also good Xylophone sound; a toy-like effect in upper register.

Hard rubber mallets—less bite to the sound, but good for general use.
Medium rubber mallets—still less bite than hard rubber mallets.
Soft rubber mallets—too soft for general use.

Hard cord mallets—less bite than plastic mallets, but good for general use.
Medium cord mallets—still less bite than hard cord mallets.
Soft cord mallets—too soft for general use, but possible for softer passages where a more subdued, Marimba-like color is appropriate.

Hard yarn mallets—more subtle. Similar to medium cord mallets.
Soft and medium yarn mallets—useless in upper register. Possible in lower octaves for soft, Marimba-like effects.

A composer wishing to be specific in his mallet designation may request any of those recommended above; otherwise he may specify only "soft," "medium," or "hard."

DISTINCTIVE FEATURES

1. The Xylophone sparkles in its higher range, especially in loud and exciting rhythmical passages. It may be used in a solo capacity or for highlighting the woodwind, brass, or high strings; but, like all percussion instruments, its usefulness in soft and subtle sections should not be overlooked.

2. Doubling melodic lines in unison or at the octave is traditional.

3. Highlighting individual notes within a motive has likewise been used to good advantage.

4. It adds accent and color to medium or high percussive chords. As many as four mallets can be used if the interval between the mallets in each hand is not over an octave, preferably not to exceed a 6th. But writing four-part harmony may present some sticking problems.[2]

5. The Xylophone is excellent used alone on short motivic solo statements in pointillistic writing.

6. "White note" glissandos add a touch of bright color and offer variety to this overused effect on the harp. "Black note" glissandos are possible, but not as effective.

7. Although the Xylophone sounds an octave higher than written, the quality is more important than the transposition.

8. Trills in seconds, thirds, fourths, etc., are possible. Notate as follows to avoid the possible misunderstanding of a trill for a roll:

Ex. 1. 1a. Trills.

Ex. 1. 1b. Trills.

9. The use of rolls for sustaining a tone in a melody, while effective, is less characteristic on the Xylophone than on the Marimba.

Ex. 1.2. Roll.

Xyl.

(But see Exs. 7.11 and 7.17)

[2]A four-mallet technique is possible on all of the mallet percussion instruments.

THE MARIMBA

(sounds as written)

Although the Marimba has been secondary to the Xylophone in the past, its subtle tone and blending capabilities have recently made it the center of attention. Its rosewood bars are slightly thinner (in relation to their length) than those of the Xylophone and are tuned to the bar's fundamental and its fourth partial. Its tone, which is amplified by resonators, includes a predominant fourth partial.

Marimbas are manufactured in numerous sizes ranging from 2 1/2 chromatic octaves to 4 1/3 chromatic octaves (actually 4 1/4 octaves). The 4-octave Marimba is the most common size at present, but the

The Marimba.

future may bring the 4 1/4-octave instrument into the number one spot. The ranges of the various sized Marimbas are as follows:

1. 2 1/2 octaves: from c^1 to f^3
2. 3 octaves: from f to f^3
3. 3 1/2 octaves: from f to c^4
4. 4 octaves. from c to c^4
5. 4 1/4 octaves: from A to c^4

The Marimba's tone varies from mellow and organ-like in the lower register to sharp and brilliant in the upper register. Its unique timbre blends well with most wind instruments, particularly the woodwinds; but its wide scope of tone quality requires a very careful choice of beaters to obtain the best possible sounds.

BEATERS[3]

Hard rubber mallets—very effective in upper register, similar to the Xylophone sound. They are harsh in lower octaves.
Medium rubber mallets—good for upper half of instrument; harsh in lower octave.
Soft rubber mallets—good general purpose mallets. Effective throughout, except for extreme upper register.

Hard cord mallets—harsh sound, similar to the Xylophone. Good in upper octaves, but harsh in lower octaves.
Medium cord mallets—not so harsh as hard cord mallets.
Soft cord mallets—excellent for general use over entire range.

Hard yarn mallets—relatively good for entire range; bring out upper notes well, but somewhat brittle in lower range.
Medium yarn mallets—good for entire range of instrument; mellow sound throughout.
Soft yarn mallets—particularly good in lower octave. Lose brilliance in upper octave and should be avoided at that end of instrument.

Brass, plastic, and wood mallets—not to be used.

DISTINCTIVE FEATURES

1. Follow the suggestions for the Xylophone.

2. The Marimba is especially warm and beautiful in soft, low passages played with soft yarn mallets either as solo or blended with other instruments of dark color.

[3]See footnote on page 4.

3. It is excellent for solo passages or in combination with other instruments. Blending is contingent upon choice of mallets.

4. The notes are often rolled unless otherwise specified, but see Exs. 7.11, 7.17 and related material in Chapter 7.

5. The volume is limited. The tone will not project through thick or loud scoring.

6. A three- or four-mallet technique is especially appropriate for the Marimba.

THE VIBE

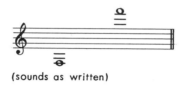

(sounds as written)

The Vibe (also known by the trade names *Vibraphone* and *Vibraharp*) is the only mallet percussion instrument utilizing a tremolo (intensity variation). The tremolo is produced by electrically-driven fans in the top of the resonator tubes. The Vibe is generally manufactured in two sizes:

1. 2 1/2 chromatic octaves: from c^1 to f^3
2. 3 chromatic octaves: from f to f^3 (shown above)

The 3-octave instrument is the one most commonly used in college and professional organizations.

With the motor turned off, the metal bars of the Vibe produce pure tones similar to that of a tuning bar. This quality blends well with winds. With the motor in operation, the tones suddenly come alive with a quality unique to the instrument. The speed of the tremolo can be varied on the newer instruments from slow to fast: from about three pulsations per second to about eight pulsations per second.

The sustained tone, so characteristic of the Vibe, is controlled by a pedal mechanism that damps *all* tones when released (up position) and

The Vibe.

lets them ring when depressed (down position). The composer indicates his intentions in the same manner as pedaling indications for the piano, or by the duration of the notes.

BEATERS[4]

Brass mallets—not to be used.

Plastic mallets—to be used only for rare special effects.

Wooden mallets—same as plastic.

Hard rubber mallets—not characteristic, but permissible.

Soft rubber mallets—not generally used on the Vibe because of the rubber's tendency to absorb bar vibrations rather than to set them into vibration.

Hard cord mallets—good, sharp, percussive sound; at times metallic sounding.

Medium cord mallets—good for general playing.

Wire brushes—produce a delicate glissando.

[4]See footnote on page 4.

Soft cord mallets—excellent for smooth legato-like sounds, but still well-punctuated.

Hard yarn mallets—similar to hard cord, but somewhat more subdued.
Medium yarn mallets—similar to medium cord, but more subdued.
Soft yarn mallets—excellent for smooth legato-like playing at normal or less than normal dynamic levels.

Slap mallets—designed originally for jazz. Give a dull slapping effect with little resonance.

DISTINCTIVE FEATURES

1. Follow same general suggestions as for Marimba, but notice the smaller range of the Vibe.

2. The Vibe may be played with motor off or on. Specify "motor on," or "motor off" in either instance.

3. The motor speed may be slow, medium, or fast. Specify: "slow fan," "medium fan," or "fast fan."

4. The Vibe blends extremely well with woodwinds, particularly Flutes and Clarinets, but will also add color to other instruments.

5. Fan speed may be varied while tone is sounding, but remember that one hand is needed for the control knob.

6. Consider the various effects which can be obtained by damping certain tones in a chord while others continue to sound. This damping can be accomplished by use of either the hand or the heads of the mallets. (See "Hand damping" and Ex. 7.31.)

7. When the electric motor is turned off (motor off), the metal fans located in the tops of the resonators may be manually placed in the vertical position to allow the tones to have full benefit of the resonators. A slight crescendo effect can be obtained if the fans are turned manually from the horizontal to the vertical position while the bar is vibrating. This merely adds the resonator's amplification to the bar's unamplified sound, thus creating a seemingly impossible percussion technique.

8. Unlike the Xylophone and the Marimba, the Vibe player will *not* roll tones unless indicated.

9. Electrical amplification systems can be used to increase the instrument's power.

10. The tone of a Vibe bar can be "bent" as follows: after striking the bar with a medium or soft mallet, slowly draw a hard mallet from about two inches in toward the end of the bar, gradually applying more pressure. This lowers the pitch approximately a quarter tone. (The damper pedal must be depressed.)

THE ORCHESTRA BELLS

(sound 2 octaves higher)

The Orchestra Bells (Glockenspiel) consist of a set of metal bars, usually made of highly-tempered steel and mounted on a frame attached to a portable case. With regard to size they are probably the most consistent of the mallet percussion instruments. They are manufactured almost exclusively in one size: 2 1/2 chromatic octaves, from g to c^3 (sounding two octaves higher than written).

The Orchestra Bells are generally played with one or two mallets; but a three- or four-mallet technique, similar to that used on the Xylophone, Marimba, and Vibe, is possible within technical limitations.

The Orchestra Bells.

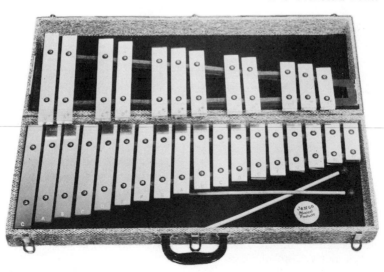

BEATERS[5]

Brass mallets—excellent for brilliant tonal effects and general playing.

Hard rubber mallets—in between brass and plastic.
Medium rubber mallets—produce à Celesta-like tone.
Soft rubber mallets—generally not used because of the rubber's tendency to absorb bar vibrations.

Plastic mallets—produce full tone but with more "click" than brass mallets.

Wooden mallets—similar to plastic mallets.

Hard cord mallets—good bell tone with less punctuation.
Medium cord mallets—limited to low dynamics.
Soft cord mallets—not recommended.

Hard yarn mallets—suitable for playing at normal volume.
Medium yarn mallets—suitable for playing at below normal volume.
Soft yarn mallets—not recommended.

DISTINCTIVE FEATURES

1. With brass mallets the Orchestra Bells have excellent carrying power over the entire orchestra—even in tutti passages.

2. Since they are so colorfully distinctive, use them with great restraint.

3. Use them for punctuating and coloring high melodic lines or chords.

4. Use for brilliant solo or short pointillistic passages. But in fast passages, the tones will run together.

5. They blend best with other metallic sounds and may be used as a substitute for the Celesta when struck with hard cord or medium rubber mallets.

6. They are a good substitute for the infrequently-found Crotales. (Suspend the proper bar from a string, passing through the hole in the bar; or place the bar on rubber bands surrounding an open cigar box. Strike with small brass mallets.)

7. The tone of Orchestra Bells sustains for some time after impact. The percussionist will automatically damp conflicting tones (if time permits) unless the composer indicates otherwise. (See Ex. 7.21 and footnote on page 108.)

[5]See footnote on page 4.

8. Although harmonics are possible, the resulting quality hardly justifies their use. (To produce harmonics, a player strikes the side of a suspended bar, or those mounted bars with exposed sides: *B*-flat, *C*-sharp, *E*-flat, and *F*-sharp. The harmonic produced is generally a slightly sharp major ninth above.)

9. A vibrato can be produced on a suspended bar by shaking, or by waving the hand back and forth over the bars; but such effects as the vibrato and harmonic should be used sparingly, if at all.

10. Like the Xylophone, the question of octave transposition is not so significant as the quality of the Bell tone.

THE CHIMES

(sound as written)

The Chimes (also called Tubular Bells) are cylindrical brass tubes of varying lengths hung on a rack and arranged in the order of a piano keyboard. The tubes are usually struck with a large rawhide mallet, and the tones may be damped with a pedal mechanism.

Chimes are commercially available in two sizes: from c^1 to f^2, and from c^1 to g^2.[6] The addition of the two top tones, however, is a relatively recent venture. Most organizations own the smaller size.

A look at the very complex harmonic and inharmonic structure of the Chime tone shows the reason for so much controversy regarding the transposition of this instrument. Since the tone is characteristic of the bell tone, it gives the typical "out-of-tune" sound, particularly when one is near the Chimes. The *strike tone*, in particular, contains many frequencies. But if c^1 (middle *C*) is struck, one hears both a predominant c^1 and c^2 with a rather strong out-of-tune sixth below. Since the character of the sound (rather than the exact pitch) is significant in scoring, the composer is advised to consider this instrument as non-transposing.

[6]The Parsifal Chimes (so named for Wagner's use of the instrument in his scoring of *Parsifal*) extend the range of the standard Chimes downward by one octave. These are no longer commercially available, although some rental firms have a few remaining sets.

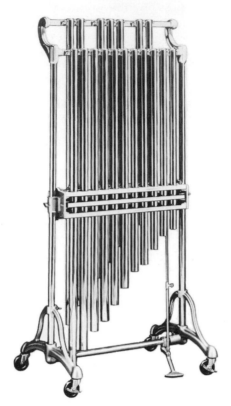

The Chimes.

BEATERS

Rawhide mallet—an all-purpose mallet which brings out all of the typical harmonics and inharmonics of the tube. It produces the best imitation of church bells. Unless otherwise specified, this mallet will be used.

Chamois or rawhide-covered mallet—for special soft effects the mallet head is often covered with chamois.

Wood mallet—used for strident fortissimo passages.

Metal mallet—like wood mallet, but more strident.

Rubber or cord mallet—good for glissandos and other special effects.

DISTINCTIVE FEATURES

1. The Chimes are traditionally used to represent church bells. They project well over the entire ensemble.

2. The Chimes are particularly effective when used to color soft chords or slow-moving melodic lines.

3. Because of the out-of-tune character of the Chimes, they are generally not used for more than two-part writing, and then only when the harmonic rhythm is relatively slow.

4. Quite rapid two-mallet technique is possible by the experienced performer, but here the damper pedal is essential. (In jazz the drummer is sometimes called upon to play a "ride" solo on the Chimes.)

5. White note glissandos are possible, black note glissandos are possible, but impractical.

THE CROTALES

(sound two octaves higher)

Although sometimes incorrectly referred to as "Finger Cymbals," the Crotales (or Antique Cymbals) are thicker and have a definite pitch. They vary in size from approximately 3 to 5 inches in diameter and are

The Crotales.

tuned to a chromatic scale with the written range extending from c^2 to c^3. Most professional orchestras own only a few of the pitches in this upper octave but will generally rent complete sets if there is sufficient time and the performance justifies the expense and inconvenience. A lower octave is manufactured today, but this set is even more rare than the upper octave and much less desirable in tone quality.

The untrained ear may easily confuse the sound of the Crotales with that of the Orchestra Bells, but some difference exists in tone quality. The sound of the Crotales seems to be more diffused and less piercing than that of the Orchestra Bells because of the design and metallic content of the plates.

Although the Crotales may be played by striking two plates of the same pitch together (described under "Finger Cymbals"), the normal practice today is to mount the individual Crotales in keyboard fashion on a rack and strike them with various beaters.

BEATERS

Same as those used for the Orchestra Bells.

DISTINCTIVE FEATURES

1. The Crotales are used in a manner similar to the Orchestra Bells, although their penetrating power is somewhat less.

2. When arranged in a mounted chromatic octave, rather rapid passages are only slightly more difficult than on the Orchestra Bells, but the tones tend to blur.

3. They blend especially well with string or harp harmonics, or with high, soft woodwinds.

4. A vibrato is possible when a single cymbal is held suspended in the hand. Specify: "vib.—obtain by shaking."[7]

[7] It is recommended in all areas of percussion notation that any effect contrary to the normal method of producing the tone be specified in terse language, rather than by coined symbols which vary with each composer. A return to the natural method is indicated by the abbreviation "nat."

The Membrane Instruments **2**

THE TIMPANI

Most college and professional musical organizations have a minimum of four Timpani—usually those shown below. The 26-inch and the 29-inch Timpani are often used interchangeably with the 25- and 28-inch Timpani. For all practical purposes, the composer may consider their ranges

The Timpani.

identical; but the larger drum will produce a fuller tone. Timpani smaller than the 23-inch (Piccolo Timpani) and larger than the 32-inch are occasionally found in college and professional orchestras; but it is best to confine the writing to those shown above, unless the composer is writing for a particular orchestra which owns the less common sizes.

The basic tuning of the Timpano is usually done by adjusting the head to a predetermined low pitch or "tuning pitch" (shown above as the lowest note available). The pedal Timpani should have the pedal in the low pitch position when tuning the head to the fundamental. This tuning pitch can be raised by various types of pedal or crank devices within the interval of a perfect fifth. This is the *practical range*, for the head tension is moderate; but the tone quality is better in the upper range. (The practical ranges are shown above in whole notes, but one new model guarantees one full octave on each drum.)

An additional major second is available on most instruments. Since this extension causes greater head tension, the tone quality will suffer; however, any drum in proper mechanical condition and with a good head should be able to reach these tones. Some drums may extend beyond the extreme ranges given, but this condition is very unpredictable and inconsistent, and composers should not request it.

On some occasions, composers are justified in using an artificial tuning: tuning a Timpano to a note lower than its usual basic tuning note; for instance, tuning the 23-inch drum to *c* rather than to *d*. This tuning change, which moves the entire compass of the drum down accordingly, should not be used consistently. Such a change alters the balance of the spring device in those Timpani which employ the balanced mechanism, thus causing pitches to move to the sharp side by themselves. This practice also proves somewhat confusing to the timpanist who often relies upon the basic tuning note to be his "home base." This is particularly true of the inexperienced timpanist—a point to remember when composing for college or high school ensembles.

In addition to the general acoustical properties of the drums, three factors govern the timbre of the Timpani: the place where the timpanist strikes the head, the type and hardness of the stick used, and muting (placing felt on the head, for example). The first of these will normally be decided by the timpanist, for he carefully chooses the spot (one-third of the radius from the rim) to produce the best tone. The composer should specify the type stick needed for the exact effect or desired blending quality. If he makes no specifications, the timpanist will choose sticks compatible with the scoring.

The Timpani are usually supplied with a pedal-tuning mechanism controlled by the foot. Changes of pitch, achieved by raising and depressing this pedal, are almost instantaneous and usually done by ear and by feel; however, some Timpani have tuning gauges on them to give the player a visual indication of the approximate pitch of the drum, still leaving the fine tuning to be done by ear. The pedal Timpani are therefore not too effective in playing rapidly changing notes on one drum, but certainly more so than hand-tuned Timpani.

Most older models and many current models smaller than 23 inches or larger than 32 inches are hand-tuned; that is, they have no pedals or tuning cranks and are tuned by turning each tension screw by hand. It is wise, therefore, to confine rapid tuning changes to the four commonly used drums, but even for these, allow five seconds if possible.

It is particularly important for the composer to determine (as soon in his scoring as possible) the number of Timpani needed. Thereafter, he must plan carefully to make his Timpani writing conform to the ranges of each drum, allowing adequate time for tuning.[1]

BEATERS

Wooden mallets—good for special hard sounds, but the pitch is less pronounced. Good for brittle precise rhythmic passages of a solo nature. Use sparingly.

Hard mallets—excellent punctuation still giving good tone production.
Medium mallets—good for general usage. Less punctuation.
Soft mallets—generally for soft, sustained rolls on low pitches.

Other—The composer will generally specify only those mallets listed above. Other satisfactory beaters include wire brushes, Maracas, Snare Drum stick, and Marimba mallets. To be used with restraint are Timpani mallets made from such materials as rubber, sponge, chamois, yarn, sheepskin, plastic, and glass, since sounds produced by these mallets can be approximated by the more conventional Timpani mallets or the MPI[2] mallets.

DISTINCTIVE FEATURES

1. The Timpani are bass instruments and therefore more effective when used on bass lines which do not move too rapidly. They are most

[1]A professional timpanist can change quite quickly and can even play melodies on one Timpano if the changes are confined to rather small intervals. Obviously he could easily change *f* to *g* on the 23-inch Timpano if he were playing on this instrument at the time. But if he were playing on the 30-inch and had to change the 23-inch from *e*-flat to *a*, it would take longer to move over to this drum and find the correct pitch. The minimum of twenty seconds should be allowed for each change of pitch on a hand-tuned drum. (See Ex. 8.2 for tuning instructions.)
[2]Mallet percussion instruments.

effective when used on exciting and animated rhythmic patterns, or on a reiterated or rolled pedal tone.

2. An adept timpanist can play simple melodies on a single Timpano by manipulating the pedal rapidly and smoothly while tuning each pitch carefully with his ear. But such melodies cannot be played rapidly since pedal changes often produce glissandos between the tones. Rapid pedal manipulation impairs accuracy of pitch. Further, two drums may cover an octave when used together; but as the timpanist leaves the range of one and begins to use that of the second drum, he must remember the last pitch played on the first drum to know what direction and to what degree to move the pedal when he returns to it. These difficulties are often overlooked by those not familiar with the instrument. Generally, however, melodic lines are best assigned to other instruments.

3. Although the Timpani are traditionally used with the brass, the tutti orchestra, or band, do not overlook their charm in soft passages.

4. The Timpani are especially potent imitating a motive previously sounded and are excellent when used in pointillistic passages with other percussion instruments.

5. It is possible to play on two Timpani at the same time. (Write stems up for the smaller Timpano and stems down for the larger, when rhythms do not agree. Otherwise both notes may be stemmed together.)

6. Rolls on two Timpani are effective. (Such rolls are smoother when two players are used.) (See Ex. 7.16.)

7. The glissando, executed by moving the pedal (or crank) after the head has been struck and while it is still vibrating, produces a peculiarly striking effect. (See Ex. 7.22.) The ascending glissando is better, for the descending glissando diminishes almost immediately after the impact, with the relaxing head tension tending to stifle vibrations. This can be artificially remedied if the timpanist will lightly tap the head with one mallet during the descending glissando, but the effect is somewhat less agreeable than that of the ascending glissando. The "natural" glissando should seldom exceed two or three seconds in duration, for head vibrations will become almost inaudible after that time. The tone can be sustained (ascending and descending) for an indefinite period so long as the timpanist continues to roll while altering the head tension.

8. A less precise pitch, and a Tom-Tom-like tone, can be produced by placing a piece of felt, a chamois, or folded handkerchief on the Timpano head. Specify: "muted."

9. A special, dead, cannon-like thud can be obtained by striking the Timpano in dead center, fortissimo. Use hard mallets.

10. Various other effects can be achieved by striking the rim or copper bowl, using a variety of beaters, dropping coins on the head, playing with the fingers or fingernails, and blowing a horn into the head. Although such devices have all been used effectively, they can be overused and should be avoided by the novice.

THE ROTO TOMS

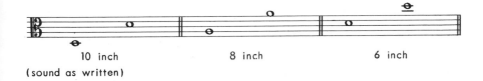

10 inch   8 inch   6 inch

(sound as written)

An exciting addition to the family of percussion instruments are the Roto Toms. These are pitched drums, similar in sound to small Timpani and available in three sizes: 10-inch, 8-inch, and 6-inch diameters.

Each Roto Tom has a usable range of one octave with a composite range of two octaves for the set of three. Constructed with a central tuning mechanism, each drum can quickly be tuned by rotating the upper rim. Tonal resonance decreases at the extreme ranges of each drum, but otherwise the tone is clear and reverberates longer than on the non-pitched Tom-Toms—approximately two seconds.

The Roto Toms.

BEATERS

Soft Timpani mallets—too soft for general usage.

Medium Timpani mallets—good tone quality, especially in the lower range.

Hard Timpani mallets—good tone quality, especially in the upper range.

Marimba mallets—very desirable, especially the yarn- and cord-wound mallets. Use the cord for the higher pitches.

Other—wooden-headed Xylophone mallets are effective where a more "wooden" sound is desired. Other sticks, mallets, and wire brushes may be used for special sounds.

DISTINCTIVE FEATURES

1. The Roto Toms may be used to extend the upper range of the Timpani although they produce somewhat less volume and resonance.

2. They may be used as a new and contrasting color among the many other percussion instruments. They are particularly desirable in chamber music groups and percussion ensembles.

3. The higher pitches of the Roto Toms might be more compatible with high brass or woodwinds than the lower pitches of the Timpani.

4. Simple melodic lines can be played on one drum, but one hand is needed for tuning. But like the Timpano, a glissando results when tunings are made before the tone decays.

5. Upward and downward glissandos are possible in the lower ranges where the heads are less tensioned.

6. Some percussionists have a set of four Roto Toms, using two of the eight-inch diameters. This makes possible the performance of four-note motives without tuning.

7. Indicate "set up" and "tuning" the same as for the Timpani. Although bass and treble clefs may be used, the alto clef is recommended.

THE SNARE DRUM

The Snare Drum has a top and a bottom head termed "batter" and "snare" head, respectively. The reason for the first term is quite obvious. The latter derives its name from the gut or wire strands strung firmly across that head. These are termed "snares."

The modern Snare Drum has a lever on the side which disengages the snares from the head, thus allowing the drum to serve as a substitute for the Tom-Tom. The smaller concert Snare Drums are often used for the Soprano Tom-Tom and the larger concert Snare Drums (or Parade Drums) for the Tenor Tom-Tom when two sizes are required.

The Snare Drums generally fall into one of three categories according to their depth and width. Moving from the smallest to the largest, we find first the "Jazz" Drum. This drum varies from 3 to 5 inches in depth (including the half-inch sizes as well) and from 13 to 14 inches in width. Next comes the "Concert" Snare Drum which varies from 5 to 8 inches in depth (including the half-inch sizes) and from 14 to 15 inches in width. The "Parade" Drum (Field, Street, or Military Drum) ranges from 10 to 12 inches in depth and from 14 to 16 inches in width. No clear-cut lines exist between Jazz and Concert Drum sizes, however, for many excellent jazz artists use the concert-sized drums, and vice-versa; but generally the characteristics of the shallow drums are high "pitch," clarity, and crispness. The deep drums offer carrying power, depth of sound, and the characteristic military sound. The following sizes[3] represent those most often used today in the three areas of drumming:

The Snare Drum.

[3]In showing the dimensions of the drums, the first figure indicates depth, the second the diameter of the drum head.

Jazz Drum: 5 by 14

Concert Drum: 5 by 14 and 6 1/2 by 14. (This order is generally the case in all schools, while the reverse is true in professional organizations.)

Parade Drum: 12 by 15 and 10 by 14

BEATERS

Snare Drum sticks—vary in size from the light jazz model sticks to the heavier Parade Drum sticks. The drummer will generally choose the proper sticks to fit the demands of the music.

Wire brushes—specified to a large extent, particularly in jazz drumming. Their characteristics are discussed in more detail below.

Other—Various sounds can be achieved with other beaters. Experiment with Timpani and MPI mallets.

DISTINCTIVE FEATURES

1. If the composer has a choice, he should specify "small," "medium," or "large" Snare Drum, or Parade Drum for the largest sizes.

2. Snare Drums will be played with snares on, unless otherwise directed by the words "snares off." The return to normal is indicated by "snares on."

3. Although the Snare Drum has traditionally been associated with military music, do not hesitate to use it in pianissimo and thinly-scored, lyrical passages.

4. A special "pistol shot" effect can be obtained by the "rim shot." The drummer plays the "rim shot" in one of three ways:
   (a) He rests one stick on hoop and head and strikes it with the shaft of the other stick;
   (b) He strikes the hoop and head simultaneously with a single stick (not always dependable);
   (c) He places the tip of one stick on the batter head and strikes the shaft with the other stick (sometimes called a "stick shot").
   It is necessary to specify only "rim shot." The drummer will determine how to play it. (See Ex. 7.9.)

5. Playing "on the rim" is a delicate and appealing sound for soft passages. (See Exs. 7.3 and 7.7.)

6. One may even specify "play on shell" (or side) of drum, but this sound will vary with the size and construction of the drum, and whether the shell is made of metal or wood.

7. If a less resonant and softer Snare Drum sound is desired, with less snare response, the composer may call for playing "near the edge." The timbre is somewhat changed and conveys the impression of the drum being played off in the distance.

8. Another less resonant but crisp sound can be obtained by the use of a drum mute, or by placing a handkerchief (a piece of felt or other cloth) on the head. Specify: "muted."

9. Single notes may be ornamented with grace notes to give tone breadth. (See Ex. 7.18.)

10. The roll is the percussionist's means of sustaining a tone and is always effective whether long, short, or combined with various rhythmical patterns. (See the sections on "the unmeasured roll" and "ornamented notes" in Chapter 7.)

11. Wire brushes are popular Snare Drum beaters. Rolls with wire brushes are generally achieved by rapid single strokes. If a composer desires an extremely soft roll, he should specify "one brush in circular motion," or use the word "stir," or "swish." To avoid misconception, the composer should include specific instructions. One possible notation is shown in Ex. 7.5. (See also Ex. 7.33.)

THE TENOR DRUM

The Tenor Drum is very similar to the Parade Drum in size and construction, but it has no snares. The Tenor Drum may vary in size from approximately 10 by 14 inches to 12 by 17 inches or larger, with the

The Tenor Drum.

12 by 17 being the most common. With the increase in size, the pitch of the drum deepens and begins to approach the sound of the Bass Drum.

The larger Tenor Drums are similar to the commercially manufactured two-headed Tom-Toms, and the Parade Drums; therefore, the percussionist will often interchange, if the need for such substitution arises. Several percussionists have indicated that in the absence of a Tenor Drum, they use the Parade Drum with snares removed (or disengaged by use of the snare release). This allows a single player to readily perform two parts on one drum, if the parts are not sounding simultaneously.

BEATERS

Snare Drum sticks—used to a great extent, particularly for Tom-Tom effects. The sound is precise and articulate and good for rapid rhythmical patterns and rolls. The use of the butt of Snare Drum sticks produces a louder and deeper sound.

Hard felt-headed mallets—the typical Tenor Drum beater as used in the marching band. The sound is less precise and articulate than with Snare Drum sticks.

Other—any type of beater may be used. The composer should acquaint himself with the various sounds produced by them.

DISTINCTIVE FEATURES

1. The Tenor Drum is used in much the same way as you might use the large concert Snare Drum or Parade Drum without snares. It is especially useful in accenting rhythmical motives in the brass or tutti orchestra.

2. A dark and somber effect can be intensified by the use of the Tenor Drum with the felt-headed sticks.

3. Such effects as the "rim shot," "near the rim," and "with brushes," may be used, but with less effectiveness than on the Snare Drum.

4. With Snare Drum sticks, any passage can be executed on the Tenor Drum that can be played on the Snare Drum, but fast, intricate rhythms tend to blur.

THE BASS DRUM

The Bass Drum is constructed much the same as the Snare Drum and Tenor Drum, but on a larger scale. (Snares, however, are not used.) Sizes vary from the small 6 by 26 up through 18 by 40 inches.

Generally, the marching bands utilize a small Bass Drum (approximately 12 by 28) while the concert organizations prefer drums 16 by 34 inches and larger. A few symphony orchestras use a single-headed drum (Gong Bass Drum) interchangeably with the conventional two-headed drum. If the composer has a specific Bass Drum sound in mind, it is wise for him to specify "large," "medium," or "small." In percussion ensembles Bass Drums of varying sizes (as well as other drums) are often used to achieve more pitch variety.

Some composers are asking that the Bass Drum be used in a horizontal position[4] to facilitate playing more intricate rhythmic patterns—

The Bass Drum.

[4]Some manufacturers are now making a Bass Drum stand which adjusts easily from the vertical to the horizontal position.

usually with Timpani or Marimba mallets; but the percussionist will turn the Bass Drum if required by the music. The volume is greater and the sound is more directional with the Bass Drum in a vertical position.

BEATERS

Snare Drum sticks—good brittle sound, but not typical.

Hard felt mallet—used for more brittle, marcato, and loud passages.

Large yarn-wound Marimba mallets—perfect for punctuation and definition. Excellent for very clear and concise rhythmic patterns which may be rapid and in need of careful articulation.

Large lamb's wool mallet—the typical Bass Drum mallet. Best used for passages not requiring speed or precise articulation.
Small lamb's wool mallet—more precise than the large lamb's wool mallet.

Other—Any of the beaters used on the Timpani or Snare Drums may be used on the Bass Drum. Each has its own character, with the softer beaters generally giving a less definite stroke, but clearer tone. The depth of tone is proportionate to the weight of the mallet.

DISTINCTIVE FEATURES

1. In the marching band, the Bass Drum is traditionally used for reinforcing the beat. It is used in this manner in orchestral and concert-band music as well as in a very musical sense when single notes or motives are very important to the character of a particular passage.

2. A sustained roll will normally be executed by playing with two matching mallets unless otherwise specified. The Bass Drum roll can be thunderous and almost overwhelming, or soft and murmuring if played with soft mallets.

3. Like the other drums, the Bass Drum can be muted. In the vertical position, this is usually done with the left hand on one head and the right knee on the other; but in the horizontal position, the Bass Drum is usually muted by placing a piece of cloth over the upper head. The tone is naturally somewhat subdued and less resonant. Isolated short tones are stopped (damped) by placing the hand(s) and/or knee on one or both heads after striking the note.

4. Singular explosive "cannon shots" can be achieved by striking the

drum in dead center. The "cannon-shot" can be varied by using different beaters.

5. The Bass Drum may be used as a large Tom-Tom in a group of several drums tuned to varying pitches.

6. For contrasting tones, a different kind of beater can be used in each hand. (See Ex. 7.6.) Also, the two heads can be tuned differently, a characteristic of Scotch drumming.

THE TOM-TOMS

The name Tom-Tom has often been a catch-all for any kind of drum without snares. Also the words "concert," "tunable,"[5] "Chinese," and "Indian" have been affixed to the name Tom-Tom. As is often the case, most of these names have ceased to have a specific meaning and are often used interchangeably for the same instrument. Only "Chinese" and "Indian" can be used to identify specific kinds of Tom-Toms, and even in the latter, one might indicate whether the reference is to American-Indian drums or to the many kinds found in India. (The American-Indian Tom-Tom and Chinese Tom-Tom are discussed separately.)

Two commercially manufactured types of Tom-Toms are available in the United States at this writing: the Two-headed Tom-Tom and the One-headed Tom-Tom. If the composer has a choice—and there is a difference in tone quality—he should specify.

The Two-headed Tom-Tom

This instrument, used extensively in both jazz and concert music, is similar in appearance and size to the Tenor Drum. Also, like the Tenor Drum, it has no snares. Although sizes vary from 8 by 12 to 20 by 18 inches, percussionists normally have available only two sizes of the several sizes listed in percussion catalogs.

[5]The use of the word "tunable" is an unfortunate choice in most instances. For instruments such as Tom-Toms, Bongos, and Conga Drums, a better word would be "adjustable." They are not tunable in the sense that Timpani are tunable. For the above instruments, this designation means only that the heads can be tensioned for approximate pitch and better tone quality. (Almost all membrane, metallic, and wooden percussion instruments have a prominent and, usually, identifiable pitch; but they are considered instruments of *indefinite* pitch and are so used in most instances.)

The Tom-Toms.

In the percussion identification chart (Ex. 8.1), the composer should generally indicate which type of Tom-Tom is wanted. Thereafter he may refer to it simply as "Tom-Tom." If he writes for two, he should specify "high" and "low." If he has no distinct preference for drum types, he may merely specify "Tom-Toms" and expect substitutions—especially when more than two are requested:

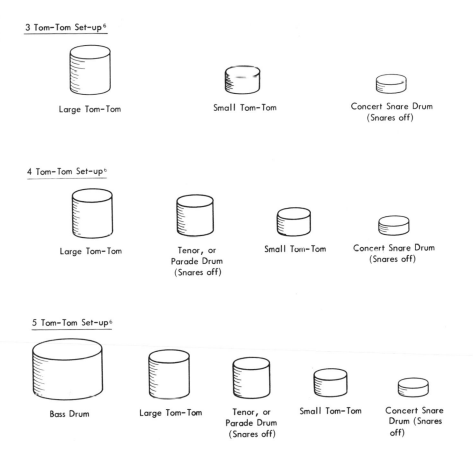

3 Tom-Tom Set-up[6]

Large Tom-Tom   Small Tom-Tom   Concert Snare Drum
                                               (Snares off)

4 Tom-Tom Set-up[6]

Large Tom-Tom   Tenor, or   Small Tom-Tom   Concert Snare Drum
                 Parade Drum   (Snares off)
                 (Snares off)

5 Tom-Tom Set-up[6]

Bass Drum   Large Tom-Tom   Tenor, or   Small Tom-Tom   Concert Snare
                              Parade Drum   Drum (Snares
                              (Snares off)   off)

BEATERS

Yarn mallets—produce an ominous, foreboding sound on the larger
instruments.

Cord mallets—similar to yarn but with more articulation, particularly
for the smaller instruments.

Hard felt Timpani mallets—good choice for a Tom-Tom tone.

Other—Snare Drum sticks, Tenor Drum mallets, and various other beaters, including Marimba mallets, may be used depending upon the
effect desired.

[6]Higher-pitched Tom-Tom sounds can be obtained by eliminating the larger
drums and using Bongos in the upper range.

DISTINCTIVE FEATURES

1. Most of the features and sticking techniques related to the other drums pertain equally well to the Tom-Tom.

2. A variety of tonal effects will be obtained by the use of various sticks and by playing dead center or near the rim.

3. The primitive Tom-Tom sound can be simulated by muting the head with a cloth. This would be a good substitute for an American-Indian Tom-Tom.

4. A primitive rhythmical pattern is best played with one stick if the tempo is not too fast. Specify: "with one stick."

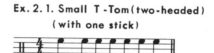

Ex. 2. 1. Small T -Tom (two-headed)
(with one stick)

The One-headed Tom-Tom

The One-headed Tom-Tom is available in varying sizes. One manufacturer lists the head sizes as 12, 13, 14, and 15 inches. This instrument, a recent addition to the drum family, fills the need for other drums in percussion ensembles. Furthermore, its tone is more resonant and definite in pitch than the tone of the Two-headed Tom-Tom.

BEATERS

Same as for the Two-headed Tom-Toms.

DISTINCTIVE FEATURES

1. The One-headed Tom-Toms may be used in the same manner as suggested for the Two-headed Tom-Toms.

2. The One-headed Tom-Toms should probably be used as indefinite-pitched instruments because of the present lack of standardization.

THE AMERICAN-INDIAN TOM-TOM

The American-Indian Tom-Tom is usually a wooden shell with calfskin or another animal skin on one or both sides. Generally the skin is thick and tensioned with sinew. This Tom-Tom has a unique but logical place among the percussion family.

American-Indian Tom-Toms are commercially available in various sizes: from 5 by 7 1/2 to 9 by 17 inches (and larger by special order) from some of the manufacturers of educational rhythm instruments. Tom-Toms are made for the tourist trade by the Indians on many of the reservations and in the pueblos. Many of these are excellent instruments. But the substitution of a Snare Drum (snares off) can be expected when one writes for this instrument.

BEATERS

Snare Drum sticks—produce less resonant but very precise tone.

Indian Tom-Tom beater—a beater with a round wooden ball on the end or a wooden stick with a hard felt or leather-covered ball.

Yarn or cord mallets—material determines sound. Generally a good choice.

The American-Indian Tom-Tom.

DISTINCTIVE FEATURES

1. The American-Indian Tom-Tom is most often used with music of a primitive character.

2. Although it is generally struck with a single stick, two sticks can be used for more intricate patterns.

3. Specify size: "small," "medium," or "large."

4. Like the Latin-American instruments, the American-Indian Tom-Toms may be used for other than indigenous music. The composer is urged to consider them in this light.

THE CHINESE TOM-TOM

The Chinese Tom-Tom is a drum varying in size from 3 by 10 inches to 16 by 18 inches. Riveted to each side of its wooden shell are thick pigskin heads, and colorful Chinese drawings ornament the drum.

These Tom-Toms are not as prevalent as during the ragtime period when they were often used as a member of the Drum Set.

BEATERS

Snare Drum sticks—used to a great extent.

Marimba mallets—all Marimba mallets may be used.

Other—any of the beaters may be used for color variety.

The Chinese Tom-Tom.

DISTINCTIVE FEATURES

1. For variety, substitute the Chinese Tom-Tom for the One-headed or Two-headed Tom-Tom.

2. The Chinese Tom-Tom is excellent for a varied timbre or pitch when combined with the other drums in motivic or antiphonal writing.

3. Like most drums, various tones may be produced by playing on different places on the head or with different beaters.

THE TAMBOURINE

Both a metallic and a membrane instrument, the Tambourine consists of a shallow wooden shell with pairs of small jingles suspended in openings in the shell. One side of the shell is covered with a calf-skin or plastic head.

Tambourines, like most percussion instruments, vary considerably in size. Although they are found in professional organizations from approximately 6 to 15 inches in diameter, the normal size is about 10 inches. They are also available with a varying number of jingles. The composer need not be concerned with size unless he has a specific effect in mind or wishes to contrast two or more sizes; in this case he should specify "small," "medium," or "large."

BEATERS

Hand, knuckles, and fingers—most commonly used, although the Tambourine is also occasionally struck against the knee.

Other—Snare Drum sticks, Marimba mallets, wire brushes, and other beaters may be used.

The Tambourine.

DISTINCTIVE FEATURES

1. The Tambourine should generally be used with restraint. Most composers would agree with Kennan when he says ". . . instruments of highly individual color are generally effective in inverse proportion to the amount they are used."[7]

2. Complex rhythmic patterns or rolls, or combinations of the two, are possible and are notated in the manner of the drums.

3. Rolls on the Tambourine are produced as follows:
   a. Shake roll: Best for higher dynamic levels, but a crescendo from piano to fortissimo can be achieved. Shake rolls may be sustained indefinitely.
   b. Thumb roll: Excellent for lower dynamic levels but also good for short, relatively loud bursts. At the pianissimo level the thumb roll should be limited to approximately three seconds.
   c. Rolls, as well as intricate rhythmic patterns, can be played with two hands (two fingers or two soft mallets) with the Tambourine placed on a felt pad on a table—head up or down. (Less drum sound results when the head is down.)

4. The Tambourine may be muted with either fingers or handkerchief. Specify: "mute with fingers," or "mute with handkerchief."

5. A Tambourine may be placed, head up, on a Timpano or other kind of drum. Striking the head of the Timpano with sticks or mallets produces a tone colored by the jingles of the Tambourine.

6. A recent use of the small Tambourine involves attaching it to the top of the Hi-Hat rod to combine the Tambourine sound with that of the Hi-Hat choke.

7. The percussionist may also play upon the Tambourine with Snare Drum sticks.

8. The Tambourine may be sounded by a combination of striking and shaking (without striking):

Ex. 2. 2. Tambourine

9. A colorful effect is obtained by placing a Tambourine, head up, on the low strings of a Grand Piano. The Tambourine may be played upon with the fingers or mallets or various patterns may be played on the Piano in the lower range.

10. See "Pandeiro."

[7]Kent Wheeler Kennan, *The Technique of Orchestration* (Englewood Cliffs, N. J.: Prentice-Hall, Inc., 1952), p. 213.

THE DRUM SET

The Drum Set is associated almost exclusively with dance, jazz, and commercial music, although symphony orchestras and concert bands have made some use of it.

Although Drum Sets may vary considerably, in terms of jazz and commercial usage, the set is reasonably well standardized. A typical Drum Set often consists of the following:

Snare Drum: 5 by 14 inches
Bass Drum: 14 by 22 inches (with foot pedal)
Two Cymbals: an 18-inch and a 20-inch[8]
Hi-Hat Cymbals: 14 inch
Two Tom-Toms (Two-headed): 9 by 13 inches and 16 by 16 inches
Cowbell

The drummer will possibly use additional percussion instruments—particularly the Latin-American instruments.

All of the instruments are arranged to be played by *one* drummer, seated. The Bass Drum and the Hi-Hat are played with foot pedals; the Bass Drum with the right foot, the Hi-Hat with the left.

The Drum Set.

[8]The smaller Cymbal is usually lighter in weight and responds more quickly. The larger Cymbal is of medium weight and is generally used for the "ride" rhythm pattern.

BEATERS

Snare Drum sticks—used almost exclusively for playing on the Snare Drum, the Tom-Toms, the Cymbals, and the Hi-Hat (in addition to the "sock" effect.)[9]

Wire brushes—also used to a great extent on Drums and Cymbals in softer music and for more legato sounds.

Marimba mallets—especially colorful when used on both Drums and Cymbals.

Other—Other beaters are used for variety, but to a much lesser degree than those listed above.

DISTINCTIVE FEATURES

1. The advantage of the Drum Set is twofold: One percussionist can (a) cover several instruments—can play at least four simultaneously—and (b) can play complex rhythms, divided between several instruments, better than when these instruments are relegated to several performers.

2. Although the Drum Set has not been used to any great extent in non-jazz groups, its use, possibly to embrace still more of a variety of instruments, is highly recommended. The forbidding problems of notation have probably been a deterrent in the use of the Drum Set. (For notational suggestions, see Exs. 7.32, 7.33, 7.34, and 7.35.)

3. Refer to the sections dealing specifically with the various instruments used in the Drum Set.

[9]See information on the Hi-Hat Cymbals.

The Metallic
Instruments   **3**

THE SUSPENDED CYMBAL

The Cymbal is a curved metal plate with a raised bell (or cup) in the center. When suspended from a cord or supported on a Cymbal stand where it is free to vibrate, it is referred to as a Suspended Cymbal.

The Suspended Cymbal.

It has three identifiable areas:

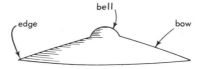

Cymbals are available in sizes ranging from approximately 10 to 24 inches[1] and in weights ranging from paper thin to extra heavy. For purpose of clarification, the sizes are grouped approximately as follows:

Small: 10 through 14 inches
Medium: 15 through 18 inches
Large: 19 through 24 inches

The tone of the thin Cymbal will respond rapidly and decay quickly. The opposite is true of the heavy Cymbal. Also, heavy Cymbals appear to have a more distinctive pitch than thin Cymbals. A small Cymbal will have somewhat the same characteristics as the thin Cymbals, while a large Cymbal will have those common to the heavy Cymbal. Combining these two factors produces various characteristics understandable only by hearing the sounds.

Keeping in mind that virtually no organization carries every size and every weight of Cymbal, the composer should specify the desired Cymbal only if he is familiar with the various types. It is generally better to specify only in terms of size. The percussionist will use a proper weight Cymbal for the best sound. (It is also possible that the conductor will request Cymbal changes.)

BEATERS

Snare Drum stick—excellent for definitive, rhythmical patterns. The Snare Drum stick is good for striking the Cymbal at the edge, on the bow, or on the bell. A distinct difference also exists when the drummer uses the tip, shoulder (or shaft), or the butt of the stick. The tip produces the most delicate sound, the butt the strongest.

Yarn Marimba or Vibraphone mallets—good for crashes and for sustaining the tone.

Timpani mallets—generally to be avoided. Many percussionists say that nothing can be done with the Timpani mallets on a Suspended Cymbal that cannot be done as well, or better, with yarn-wound Marimba mallets.

Wire brushes—excellent legato effect in soft passages.

Triangle beater—colorful if a strongly metallic sound is desired.

---

[1]Cymbals smaller than 10 inches and larger than 24 inches are commercially available, but the larger sizes are not recommended—even by their manufacturers. The smaller sizes are generally relegated to the educational rhythm instrument group.

DISTINCTIVE FEATURES

1. The Cymbals are too colorful to use frequently. But use them for soft sections as well as for climaxes.

2. If the Suspended Cymbal is struck at the edge, the tone will be very broad, will last long, and will contain more of the lower partials. (Specify: "at the edge.") If the Cymbal is struck on the bow, the sound will be rather metallic and will contain more of the upper partials of the series. (Specify: "on the bow.") If struck directly on the bell, the sound will be very metallic, will have almost no sustaining ring, and its tone will sound somewhere between the tone produced by a Triangle and a Cowbell struck with a small wooden beater. (Specify: "on the bell.")

3. Rolls on the Suspended Cymbal with yarn Marimba mallets create a colorful effect particularly characteristic of the Impressionist school. The rolled crescendo is especially exciting. Because of the natural and gradual decay of tone, a diminuendo (after a crescendo roll to a climax) may be achieved as follows:

Ex. 3.1.

($\quad$ =80)

Lg. Sus. Cym. (Yrn. Mba. mal.)

(A forte-piano attack can be achieved in a similar fashion.)

4. As the percussionist can obtain a variety of pitches by using various-sized drums, so too can he obtain various pitches on the metallic instruments, particularly the Cymbals. Look for opportunities to use various sized Cymbals antiphonally (specify: "small," "medium," or "large"), or to use a rhythmic pattern which utilizes the different pitches available on *one* Cymbal. (See Exs. 7.4 and 7.8.)

5. Dragging a Triangle beater (or a coin) across the Cymbal from near the bell to the edge produces a novel sound. Although this is normally used only in soft thinly-scored passages, it is extremely colorful and is another reminder that percussion instruments can be used in quiet passages to good advantage.

6. A sound, similar to 5 above, can be obtained by sliding a long file or threaded rod along the edge of the Cymbal, but a good Cymbal hardly deserves this kind of treatment.

7. A Suspended Cymbal may be used as a poor substitute for the Hi-Hat Cymbals. If the composer wants the typical Hi-Hat sound of open versus closed Cymbals, the Cymbal's vibration is stopped with the free hand on the appropriate beats (as when the Cymbals are closed by the pedal on the Hi-Hat), and released on all others. A possible notation is shown in Ex. 7.28.

8. A high-pitched "sizzling" sound can be obtained by placing a small coin on the bow or by applying a small metal rod or coin to the edge after setting the Cymbal into vibration.

THE HAND CYMBALS

The Hand Cymbals (or Crash Cymbals) consist of two Cymbals held one in each hand and struck together with a glancing blow. Most professional organizations use a pair of 18-inch medium-weight Hand Cymbals, but they often carry two or more additional pairs of different sizes and weights. With Hand Cymbals, the composer rarely specifies sizes,

The Hand Cymbals.

although he may do so if he wishes a particular sound, limiting his choice to "small," "medium," and "large," and leaving the weights to the performer. The percussionist will generally choose the best pair among those available to match the Cymbals to the scoring.

DISTINCTIVE FEATURES

1. Although the Hand Cymbals are generally used in the fortissimo climax, they may also be used in pianissimo passages. Like the Suspended Cymbals they should be saved for special occasions and not overused.

2. The short, damped Cymbal crash is used to reinforce an accented chord. The composer should show the exact duration of the Cymbal crash, and the percussionist will use the proper damping technique to observe this. (See Ex. 7.21.)

3. Crashes which are to continue for indeterminate lengths (or until the sound decays) should be indicated by the "half tie," or the instruction "let ring," or "l.v." (let vibrate or *laissez vibrer*). Obviously the half tie is the simplest of these alternatives and is well-understood today. (See Ex. 7.21.)

4. Although the roll is generally assigned to the Suspended Cymbal, it is possible (for a special effect) on the Hand Cymbals at medium or low dynamic levels by rubbing the edges of the plates against each other. Specify: "two plate roll," or "rubbed together."

5. An interesting but little-known effect, the vibrato, can be obtained on the Hand Cymbals. Specify: "vib.—obtain by moving to and fro after striking."

6. For a soft, short "roll," the Hand Cymbals can be held together and then moved apart with a sliding motion. (See Ex. 7.13.)

7. Another soft "swish" sound can be created by holding one Cymbal in a vertical position and pushing the edge of the other plate from the bell outwards, inside the plate. Specify: "swish," or "*zischend.*"

8. A special "choke" sound can be produced by "clapping" the Cymbals together and holding them in that position following impact. This type of choke is different from the choking or damping produced by pulling the plates against the chest. To indicate this, specify: "choke and hold together."

THE SIZZLE CYMBAL

Sizzle Cymbals are available in a variety of sizes, are made in varying degrees of thickness and, in contrast to all other Cymbals, have metal rivets loosely installed in holes drilled around the circumference of the Cymbal. When the Sizzle Cymbal is struck, its natural vibrations cause the rivets to bounce, thus producing a shimmering or sizzling effect.

The Sizzle Cymbal.

BEATERS

The same variety of beaters may be used on the Sizzle Cymbal as on all other Cymbals. The Snare Drum stick is probably the most used.

DISTINCTIVE FEATURES

1. The Sizzle Cymbal is best for single strokes since the sizzling effect created by the bouncing rivets tends to obscure a complex rhythmic pattern.

2. The Sizzle Cymbal is appropriate when used with high woodwind or string trills.

3. Like the Suspended Cymbal, the Sizzle Cymbal can be damped by the free hand.

4. Rolls with Marimba mallets are effective. (See discussion under "Suspended Cymbals.")

5. The Sizzle Cymbal may be played on the bell or on the bow, as well as at the edge.

6. Various sounds may be achieved by using wire brushes and other beaters.

THE HI-HAT

The Hi-Hat (Sock, or Foot Cymbals) is usually associated with the Drum Set. It consists of a pair of 13 to 15 inch Cymbals mounted on a vertical rod manipulated by a foot pedal. The drummer brings the upper Cymbal down on the lower plate to produce a "chick" type of sound.

In the dance band or jazz combo, the drummer usually operates the Hi-Hat on the weak beats of the measure, but many jazz musicians deviate considerably from this pattern.

The Hi-Hat.

BEATERS

Although the Hi-Hat is played primarily with the foot mechanism, it can be struck with the same variety of beaters as the Suspended Cymbal.

DISTINCTIVE FEATURES

1. To obtain the typical jazz effect, the composer may write a simple basic beat and indicate by "ad lib." that improvisation is wanted. (This instruction is obviously not necessary for the jazz drummer— only when writing for the less experienced percussionist who is not jazz oriented.) But often, even in jazz drumming, an *exact* notation is needed. (See Exs. 7.32, 7.33, and 7.34.)

2. The "chick" type of sound is effective with short, staccato chords in the brass or woodwinds.

3. This effect may also serve as a grace note to a dead "thud" (sfz) on the Bass Drum, if the Drum Outfit is used.

4. The drummer often plays on the upper Cymbal with a Snare Drum stick while continuing to operate the pedal in the above-mentioned manner with the resulting sounds being either very staccato (when the Cymbals are closed) or more sustained (when the Cymbals are open.) (A possible notation is shown in Ex. 7.35.)

5. Playing on the bell and on the bow are common.

6. With the two plates drawn almost together with the foot pedal, the Cymbals give a particularly interesting sizzling sound when struck with a Snare Drum stick. The sound will carry well over heavy scoring.

7. With a piece of heavy cardboard held between the closed Cymbals, a unique sound can be achieved by playing on the edge of the cardboard with Snare Drum sticks. The drummer sometimes uses this as a substitute for the Maraca sound.

THE FINGER CYMBALS

The Finger Cymbals, small, paired, metal plates approximately two inches in diameter, should not be confused with the Crotales which are of much higher quality and definite in pitch. Individually, each of the Finger Cymbals approximates a definite pitch, but when two mated Cymbals are struck together, the two pitches will merge and create a more indefinite-pitched ring. Like the Triangle, the sound allies itself with any tonal structure.

The Finger Cymbals.

BEATERS

Finger Cymbals can be struck with metal, wood, plastic, or other beaters.

DISTINCTIVE FEATURES

1. The Finger Cymbals, like the Triangle, Orchestra Bells, or other soft metallic-sounding instruments, blend well with high sonorities and add an ethereal or Near-East quality to such sounds.

2. Use them where the small, high-pitched, and delicate sound is desired.

3. Although the roll is possible (with small Triangle beaters, for example), it should generally be avoided.

THE TAM-TAM

The Tam-Tam is a large circular piece of heavy hammered metal, generally having a flanged edge around its circumference to give it the look of a shallow metal bowl. It is hung by a chord strung through its rim and suspended on a metal frame. It is usually struck with a special Tam-Tam beater.

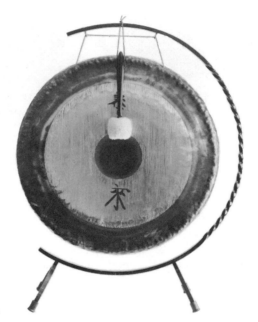

The Tam-Tam.

Most percussion manufacturers in the United States consider the Tam-Tam and the Gong as one and the same instrument, but many percussionists, notably Frederick Fennell, Paul Price, Gordon Peters, and Al Payson favor a distinction between these two. Gordon Peters, in his "Treatise on Percussion,"[2] writes:

> The fixed-pitched instruments are rightfully called "gongs" and are used throughout the Asian-Oriental cultures. They are used either singly or in sets and are suspended by a cord or rest upon a stand or on the ground.

[2]Gordon B. Peters, "Treatise on Percussion" (Master's thesis, Eastman School of Music, 1962), pp. 119–120.

The gong is essentially a bell and is made of similar alloys. In China large gongs play a prominent part in the temple music. In the form of plates (squared shapes) they are occasionally mounted in series on an upright frame. In Burma and Siam small circular gongs are mounted in series in the circular frame with the player sitting in the middle; collectively, these are popularly called a "gong-piano."

In China particularly there are also non-fixed-pitch gongs made as well. These are the types that made their way west and came eventually to be used in Western music. The Europeans began calling them "tam-tams," for what reason, no one seems to know. . . . Some prefer to call tuned metal plates "gongs," and the non-tuned "tam-tams." Some persons call the Chinese non-pitched instruments "gongs," and the Turkish ones, "tam-tams."

. . . with orchestration books and orchestration teachers each giving their own interpretations, the "semantic-gong" problem ever grows.

Al Payson in an article in *The Ludwig Drummer*[3] says:

The tam-tam, like the cymbal, has no definite pitch. The gong, which is a native of Java and Bali, has a quite discernible pitch, and it is tuned to a definite note of the scale. The gong has a raised center bulge and a side lip or flange. In this country the tam-tam has been erroneously referred to as the gong for so long that the two terms have become synonymous, particularly among composers. Hence, when the percussion part calls for gong, the tam-tam is almost always the instrument intended.

In a recent letter, Mr. Toomas Paiste (of M. M. Paiste & Sohn, makers of Cymbals, Gongs, and Tam-Tams) writes:

The correct designation is:

1. A Gong is an instrument which is tuned to a certain tone.

2. A Tam-Tam is an instrument which is tuned to a certain sound-character.

Although a few of the definite-pitched Gongs are available in symphonic organizations (and some chromatic sets available on rental), these instruments are too rare to be used by the composer today. In the interest of semantics—and the hope that the future will see a more extended use of the definite-pitched Gongs—the authors recommend using the term "Gong" for the instrument of *definite* pitch, and the use of the word "Tam-Tam" for the instrument of *indefinite* pitch. Only the Tam-Tam is discussed here.

Tam-Tam sizes generally vary between about 20 and 60 inches in diameter; however, sizes over 36 inches are rarely available.

[3] Al Payson, "Playing Techniques of the 'Secondary' Instruments," *The Ludwig Drummer*, Fall, 1963, Vol. 3, No. 2, p. 23.

BEATERS

Tam-Tam beater—nothing need be specified if the special Tam-Tam beater is used. Deviations from this, however, need to be specified.

Other—the Tam-Tam may be struck with Marimba mallets, Timpani mallets, Snare Drum sticks, Triangle beaters, wire brushes, and even the tips of the fingers.

DISTINCTIVE FEATURES

1. Like most percussion instruments, the Tam-Tam has too often been restricted to loud climactic passages. Here it is thunderous and sounds through the heaviest scoring.

2. A soft stroke or a soft sustained roll on the Tam-Tam adds a solemn or mysterious character to the music, a vague sound whose point of origin is indiscernible. The duration of the tone is exceptionally long.

3. Other sounds can be achieved with varying kinds of beaters. Describing an arc on the Tam-Tam with a Triangle beater, or drawing it from the center outwards, has been used. (It is worth repeating that the percussion instruments can be used for other than noise makers!)

4. The composer may specify Tam-Tam sizes: "small," "medium," or "large." If no sizes are specified, the percussionist will choose the appropriate Tam-Tam or will use the one available.

5. A "Water Gong" effect can be produced by partially submerging a vibrating Tam-Tam in a tub of water, thereby "bending" its tone downward in pitch.

6. An effect similar to Distinctive Feature Number 8, under "The Suspended Cymbal" can be obtained.

THE TRIANGLE

The Triangle is a round metal rod bent in the shape of a triangle with a small opening at one of the angles. It is generally struck with a metal beater. It is available in small (6-inch), medium (8-inch), and large (10-inch) sizes, but many percussionists have sizes both smaller and larger than these. It is better to indicate "high," "medium," or "low," (rather than "small," "medium," or "large") since the pitch is not only related to the size, but also to the diameter of the bar and even to the place where the bar is struck.

The Triangle.

The Triangle is a highly colorful instrument which, because of a multiplicity of overtones, tends to blend with the sonority with which it is employed.

BEATERS

Metal beater—the beater most commonly used. (These generally vary from approximately 1/16 to 5/16 inches in diameter.) The larger the beater, the larger and more brilliant the tone; but there is hardly any problem in making the Triangle sound penetrate. The small metal beaters are more desirable for intimate, soft passages, but the percussionist will use the appropriate metal beater if not specified. The sound is brilliant and metallic.

Plastic mallet—somewhat softer but with more "click" than the metal beaters.

Snare Drum stick—a Snare Drum stick or the handle of a Marimba mallet produces a smooth sounding, legato ring.

DISTINCTIVE FEATURES

1. A Triangle adds brilliance to a tutti climax or supplies a tinkling charm to soft strings or woodwinds in the upper register.

2. Not only single, but ornamented notes are possible, all ranging in volume from pianissimo to fortissimo. For rapid passages, two beaters may be used, but a composer must use good judgment in writing rapid patterns since tone decay is slow and can cause some lack of clarity.

3. Rolls are generally produced with one beater moved rapidly in an inside angle of the Triangle. (Rolls are notated the same as for other percussion instruments.)

4. A less penetrating sound comes from touching the Triangle with one hand while striking with a beater in the other. Specify: "mute with hand."

5. A vibrato may be obtained on the Triangle (similar to the Hand Cymbal vibrato). Specify: "Vib.—Strike and shake."

6. The use of appropriate-sized, metal beaters is perhaps as important as the size of the Triangle. Specify: "thin," "medium," or "thick" metal beater; otherwise the percussionist will make a choice.

THE BRAKE DRUM

As the name implies, the Brake Drum is an automobile part. It probably infiltrated the percussion ensemble after someone found that it had a rather clear and resonant tone. Although it should be considered as an instrument of indefinite pitch, very clear, bell-like tones are possible, depending upon the striking spot. Occasionally a percussionist will tune a Brake Drum to a specific pitch with the use of a grinding wheel, but the composer generally is advised to specify only relative sizes. He must realize that only about one-third of the professional or college organizations have Brake Drums. Since the automobile industry is the sole manufacturer of Brake Drums, the percussionist must either rent them, or buy them from an automobile parts dealer.

The Brake Drum tone is produced by striking it with mallets either

The Brake Drum.

on the *back* (the large part of the brake drum which is bolted to the wheel) or on the *ring* (the part where the brake lining rides). It may be suspended (to sound more resonant and with a slower tone decay) or placed on a pad on the table (to sound less resonant and with a faster tone decay).

In percussion ensembles Brake Drums are often used in sets of three, four, or five.

BEATERS

Metal Bell mallets—produce a strong bell-like tone with many high overtones.

Small metal hammer—similar to above.

Marimba mallets—produce a more mellow tone depending upon the degree of hardness of mallets.

DISTINCTIVE FEATURES

1. Like all percussion instruments, the Brake Drum may reinforce and color chords or isolated notes, especially those in the higher register.

2. Although more than one pitch can usually be obtained on *one* Brake Drum (when struck on the *back* and *ring*), variable pitches are best obtained by using Brake Drums of different sizes. Specify: "high," "medium," or "low."

3. Single notes, fast rhythmic patterns, and rolls are all possible; but some blurring of tones occurs in rapid, reiterated notes unless muting is specified.

4. Make use of the possible antiphonal effects available between Brake Drums and other percussion instruments, or between Brake Drums of different sizes.

THE ANVIL

Percussion manufacturers are now making an instrument to duplicate the sound of the old blacksmith's anvil. Although only a few of the professional and college organizations own one, a large steel or iron bar (or a length of train rail) can usually be found. In all instances, the instrument is referred to as an Anvil.

A composer should preferably call for only one size Anvil and certainly not more than three sizes. If various sizes are used, specify: "small," "medium," and "large."

BEATERS

Metal hammers—the usual beater for the Anvil.

Wooden mallets—large wooden mallets may be used for softer effects.

The Anvil.

DISTINCTIVE FEATURES

1. Like most of the seldom-used percussion instruments, the Anvil is primarily used for coloristic purposes, particularly in program music where the sound of the blacksmith's anvil is required; but there is no reason a wider and more contemporary use of the Anvil cannot be exploited.

2. The Anvil is better in loud passages but can be used in softer passages to good advantage.

3. It is often used to simulate battle sounds.

THE BELL PLATE

The Bell Plate is a flat piece of untuned steel suspended and struck with a variety of mallets. Although found in various sizes, one commercial model is 7 by 9 by 1/8 inches. When struck with a steel mallet, it sounds similar to a fire bell or train bell.

Since it is a relatively inexpensive instrument to buy, and not too difficult to make, it is found in about 75 percent of professional orchestras and 50 percent of college orchestras. It should be considered an instrument of indefinite pitch and used like the Brake Drum.

The Bell Plate.

BEATERS

Steel Bell Plate mallet—produces a harsh bell-like tone.

Wooden mallet—less impact with approximately the same bell-like tone.

Marimba mallets—resulting tone depends upon type and hardness of
mallet.

DISTINCTIVE FEATURES

1. Like all bells, the single tone is most effective: brilliant and colorful.

2. A sound similar to the fire alarm is produced by a two-mallet roll
with steel Bell Plate mallets.

3. For variety consider uses similar to those associated with the Brake
Drums and Cymbals.

THE SLEIGH BELLS AND ANIMAL BELLS

The various kinds and sizes of Sleigh Bells and Animal Bells are so
varied as to defy description. Some percussionists have the authentic
Sleigh Bells, suspended on straps, while others use commercial, paddle-

The Sleigh Bells and Animal Bells.

mounted Sleigh Bells. These may be found in several sizes; and, though the individual bell is considered indefinite in pitch, some rental shops stock complete sets of *tuned* Sleigh Bells.

Animal Bells, including Elephant Bells, Water Buffalo Bells, and Camel Bells, have found their way into the percussion ensemble in recent years. Each of these bells has its own peculiar sound depending upon design, kind, and amount of metal employed, and the number of bells used in a set. Practically all professional and college organizations own Sleigh Bells of undetermined sizes, but the Animal Bells are considerably more rare.

One should not be misled by the bell's name, for the bells are in no way proportionate in size to the animals they adorn. The Elephant Bells, for instance, are quite small, for many of them border the cloths thrown over the animal's back. The Elephant Bell has, in fact, a very delicate and musical tone.

Unless otherwise specified—as is the case of the "tuned" bells—the Sleigh Bells (and many of the Animal Bells) are found in sets with a resulting multiple-bell sound.

DISTINCTIVE FEATURES

1. Although most of these bells, particularly the Sleigh Bells, have been used primarily in descriptive music, they can be most effective in creating a jingling and sparkling color when combined with high dissonant scoring.

2. Parts for Sleigh Bells are usually limited to simple rhythms because of the difficulty in managing the instrument.

3. One might wish to be optimistic enough to specify a set of high, medium, or low Sleigh Bells. (They are available!)

4. Quite often the composer will have a particular bell sound in mind but will be dissatisfied with the conventional bells at his disposal. At this spot the various Animal Bells can be useful, for they produce every type of bell sound from a delicate "ting" to a low-pitched, unmusical "clank." To be understood properly, they must be heard.

The Wooden
Instruments 4

THE WOOD BLOCK

The Wood Block is a rectangular piece of hard wood, varying in size from approximately 1 1/2 by 6 1/4 inches to 2 1/2 by 7 1/2 inches. In most models slits are hollowed out near the playing surfaces, from both sides, to produce two different pitched tones; however, it is difficult to reverse the instrument and play on both sides in rapid passages. Therefore, it is better to use two Wood Blocks for contrasting pitches. The Wood Block, usually available in two or three sizes in most professional and college organizations, produces a dry, high-pitched, wooden sound, as one would expect. It should be considered an instrument of indefinite pitch.

The Wood Block.

BEATERS

Snare Drum sticks—the typical Wood Block sound, dry and crisp, varying with the size of the sticks and depending upon whether the tip, shaft, or butt of the stick is used. Good for intricate rhythms.

Marimba mallets—generally less wooden in sound, but equally effective, depending upon the sound desired, with the harder mallets being more penetrating and brittle. Good for single isolated notes.

Other—wooden and plastic mallets produce a sharp, brittle sound.

DISTINCTIVE FEATURES

1. Both single notes and rolls are possible on the Wood Block.

2. Its tone has a very short duration, but is penetrating.

3. The Wood Block may reinforce short dissonant chords in the brass. It is similar to the effect of the rim shot on the Snare Drum.

4. In using more than one Wood Block, specify: "high" and "low," or "high," "medium," and "low." Even in using one Wood Block, a high or low block may be specified.

THE TEMPLE BLOCKS

The Temple Blocks[1] comprise a set of five clam-shaped wooden blocks, usually brilliantly lacquered and mounted on a stand where they can achieve maximum resonance when struck. Although the five blocks are tuned to approximate the black-note pentatonic scale, this percussion instrument is considered one of indefinite pitch and so notated—usually on the five lines of the staff with the neutral clef sign, the highest pitch corresponding to the top line.

The mellow, resonant "clop" sound, produced by the Temple Blocks, is one that can hardly be duplicated by any other percussion instrument. The closest approach to it is the large Wood Block struck with a soft Marimba mallet. But a composer does not need to worry about substitutes since Temple Blocks are found in almost all professional and college organizations.

[1]The names for both the Wood Blocks and the Temple Blocks have been so confused by prefixing the words "Chinese," "Korean," and "Oriental," that these prefixes should be dropped and the instruments called only "Wood Blocks" (for the rectangular-shaped blocks) and "Temple Blocks" (for those discussed above).

The Temple Blocks.

BEATERS

Marimba mallets—any mallets used on the Marimba may be used on the Temple Blocks. The harder mallets will naturally give a more brittle and less mellow tone.

Wood, plastic, metal—generally not to be used because of the damage that will occur to the blocks.

DISTINCTIVE FEATURES

1. The single Temple Block may be used much the same as the Wood Block or any number up to five may be used for varying pitch patterns.

2. Although one tends to relate the sound of the Temple Blocks to horses' hoofs, they should not be limited to such programmatic treatment. They are appropriate for music with Oriental or primitive sounds but are equally effective for more avant-garde effects.

3. Rolls on single or multiple blocks may be used, but rolls on more than two blocks generally require more than one performer.

4. The Temple Blocks are excellent for antiphonal effects with such other percussion instruments as Tom-Toms, Bongos, Timpani, and Cowbells.

5. Should there be the need to specify the use of particular blocks, identify 1, 2, 3, 4, 5 with "1" being the largest.

THE CASTANETS

Castanets are small spoon-shaped shells, usually made from hard wood, and commercially available in three styles:

The Hand Castanets. A pair is held in each hand and clicked together wtih the fingers. A male pair of slightly lower pitch is held in the left hand while the female pair is held in the right. The Hand (or Finger) Castanets require not only considerable skill, but also sufficient time to bring into playing position. Percussionists in orchestras or bands practically never use these.

The Paddle-mounted Castanets. Here one pair of Castanets is mounted on a paddle sounding board (or handle). Most organizations will have the Paddle-mounted Castanets available. They are especially good for loud rolls or passages where extreme volume (without the need of good articulation) is required.

The Machine (or Concert) Castanets. More recently two pairs of Castanets have been mounted on a board, with the lower Castanets stationary and connected to the upper Castanets by springs. Or single Castanets may strike a rosewood board. The upper Castanets are clicked against the lower ones (or against the hardwood board) with the first fingers of the hands or with soft mallets.

DISTINCTIVE FEATURES

1. Almost any rhythmic figure[2] can be executed on the Castanets, although the player may have to use Paddle Castanets, Machine

[2]Additional information and typical Spanish dance rhythms may be found in: Al Payson, "Castanets in Modern Setting," *International Musician*, April 1963, p. 32.

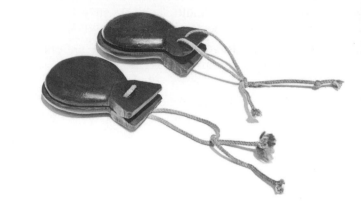

The Hand Castanets.

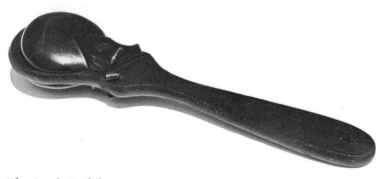

The Single Paddle Castanets.

The Machine Castanets.

Castanets, or a combination of both to perform the more intricate ones. This decision, however, is best made by the percussionist and need not concern the composer. Merely specify: "Castanets."

2. Rolls of long duration are possible and are written in the traditional manner. Ornamentations, as used in snare drumming, may be incorporated.

3. Castanets offer a welcome substitute for the Snare Drum when doubling and reinforcing the rhythm of muted brass or pizzicato strings. Imagine the substitution of Castanets for Snare Drum in Ex. 7.23, with the Trumpets muted.

4. It is difficult to disassociate the sound of the Castanets from the typical Spanish rhythm, but if used wisely, the Castanets have a rare rhythmic charm. A creative approach in their use will no doubt prove profitable and artistic in the writing of new music.

THE SAND BLOCKS

Sand Blocks are nothing more than "hand-sized" blocks of wood covered with sandpaper, their sound produced by sliding one block over the other or bringing the blocks sharply together. Since the coarseness of the sandpaper blocks affects the volume and general pitch of the sound, it is sometimes wise to specify "fine," "medium," or "coarse."

Since the "soft-shoe dancer" sound is familiar, further description is unnecessary. Notation for the Sand Blocks is the same as for other percussion except that the sliding effect is notated as a roll.

The Sand Blocks.

DISTINCTIVE FEATURES

1. The Sand Blocks are best used for less complex rhythmic patterns.

2. Rolls of all lengths are possible. Since short notes may be achieved by bringing the blocks sharply together, or by an extremely short "press" roll, care must be used to distinguish between the two:

as opposed to

♪

3. The Sand Blocks may be used in a manner similar to the Guiro, Maracas, Chocallo, wire brushes on the Snare Drum, etc.; but in each instance the sound is somewhat different.

THE SLAPSTICK

The Slapstick is another "sound-effect" instrument. The commercial Slapstick is a paddle of hard wood fastened to another hinged paddle controlled with a strong spring. Because of its construction, the Slapstick can produce only single strokes which cannot be executed too rapidly.

The Slapstick.

DISTINCTIVE FEATURES

1. Although generally used to simulate the sound of a cracking whip, or slap, the Slapstick emphasizes a climactic point or reinforces short, staccato chords in the wind or brass.

2. For variety it can be used as a substitute for the Snare Drum rim shot, or a single accented note on the Wood Block.

3. Some imaginative thinking readily provides numerous other uses for the Slapstick in contemporary scoring.

THE RATCHET

The Ratchet consists of a simple frame with several strips of wood or metal which drag along a rotating paddle wheel or cog. This instrument, which sounds somewhat like the winding of a large clock, belongs to the category of sound effects. The Ratchet is used for both short and long rolls, notated the same as for other percussion instruments. The single note is risky.

DISTINCTIVE FEATURES

1. The Ratchet is best used for loud passages. It has little dynamic range.

2. The Ratchet should be used with great restraint, even in the percussion ensemble.

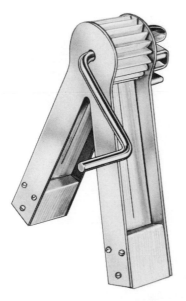

The Ratchet.

THE LOG DRUM

The present-day Log Drum is primarily of Mexican-Indian and African origin. The Aztecs called the drum a *Teponaxtle* or *Teponatzli*. These may be seen in several sizes in some of the museums in Mexico. The Teponaxtle is basically a hollowed log with two tongues of different lengths, free to vibrate when struck with a mallet.

The African "Slit Drum," which varies only slightly in construction from the Teponaxtle, is known by a variety of names depending upon place of origin and the size of the instrument. Two commonly used names are *ekwe* and *okwa*.[3] Two tones[4] are produced by striking the

The Teponaxtle Drum.

The African "Slit Drum."

[3]For more detailed information see: W. W. Echezona, "Ibo Musical Instruments in Ibo Culture" (Doctoral thesis, Michigan State University, 1963), pp. 57–66.
[4]The Ibos can produce more than two pitches on one drum. *Ibid.*, pp. 62–63.

drum on either side of the slit. The pitch difference results from the thickness of the walls of the sides of the drum.

Both types of drums produce two well-focused pitches whose intervallic relationship is usually the third, perfect fourth, or perfect fifth. But the composer should consider the Log Drum as an instrument of indefinite pitch; and he should not assume that the instrument is available, even in professional orchestras. This is unfortunate, for the tone produced by a well-made Log Drum is a beautiful and sonorous wood drum sound. (Log Drums are available in commercial versions to a limited extent, usually from the manufacturers of educational rhythm instruments, or they can be made from special woods selected for their resonance.)

BEATERS

Marimba mallets—medium rubber or medium yarn probably the most effective on the Log Drums.

Other—the African Slit Drum is almost invariably struck with a soft wood stick.

DISTINCTIVE FEATURES

1. Like the Bongos, the Log Drum should be considered as an instrument of indefinite pitch and written on two spaces: high and low.

2. Its use is similar to that of other percussion instruments: the Temple Blocks, Tom-Toms, and Timbales.

3. Write for the Log Drum only if it is available or if you cue it for Bongos, Tom-Toms, or Timbales.

The Latin-American
Instruments　**5**

One group of percussion instruments has found its way into serious American music through the popular music of the Latin-American bands and has had an increasing impact upon present-day writing for percussion, particularly upon music influenced by jazz.

Most of these instruments adapt well to multiple pitch patterns, a challenge to the composer who might wish to notate these effects. But in the style of the Latin-American dances, the performers improvise or play a stylized one- or two-measure riff. (Refer to a book on Latin-American rhythms when writing in this idiom.)

One interesting but confusing problem concerns the wide variety of names associated with some of these instruments. Whereas most of the names originate from the Spanish, Portuguese, or Indian languages, others no doubt come from incorrect spellings and the coining of trade names by percussion manufacturers. Those in this chapter appear to be the most commonly used in the United States.

THE BONGOS

The Bongos come attached in pairs: large and small, generally tuned to the interval of a perfect fourth or fifth. Although the sizes of the pairs vary somewhat, all are sufficiently small to be placed between the knees where they are generally held in playing. (They are usually mounted on a stand for concert performance.)

These drums have one head. They are available with either adjust-

The Bongos.

able heads (Tunable Bongos[1]) or nonadjustable heads, the former being preferred. The Bongos, traditionally played with the fingers, are rather difficult to play and require a highly developed and specialized technique. The accomplished Bongo player has developed exceptionally well-muscled and calloused fingers. The inexperienced Bongo player, however, has developed neither the finger muscles nor the callouses and is therefore not capable of executing artistic solo work in the traditional manner. In spite of this, the composer may assume that at least one percussionist in the section is quite familiar with the instrument and able to execute relatively involved passages.

In the true Latin-American setting, the Bongo part is most often indicated by a "chart" which shows breaks, solos, and rhythmic patterns to be reinforced. The Bongo player then ad libs within the limitations and guidelines of this chart. The composer might wish to write a more simple score and indicate by the words "ad lib" that the Bongo player may improvise beyond the patterns specified. Indeed, the Bongos are capable of so many sounds that accurate notation is very difficult. Notes for the two Bongos (high and low) are written on the staff. A good choice would be spaces two and four.

Many degrees of pitch and tonal range are possible by using various fingers on all areas of the drum head. Pressure of a free hand on various parts of the head makes possible a wide range of relative pitches on even one of the drums.

[1]See footnote under "Tom-Toms," p. 35.

BEATERS

Fingers—although striking the Bongos with the fingers is the traditional mode of playing, it is best to so indicate ("with the fingers") since percussionists will normally use cane sticks in concert music.

Cane sticks—if a more brittle sound is desired, specify "cane sticks." (Cane sticks wrapped in adhesive tape approximate the actual finger sound very closely.)

Other—Marimba and Vibe mallets are sometimes used, although the sound is not authentic.

DISTINCTIVE FEATURES

1. Everyone is familiar with the sound of the "tense" roll and the spicy Latin-American rhythms as played on the Bongos.

2. Rim shots, played with the finger striking the edge of the head, are perhaps more effective in certain situations on the Bongos than on the Snare Drums. (For notation, see "Rim Shot," Chapter 7.)

3. The Bongos usually have the most intricate rhythmic patterns of all the Latin-American instruments.

4. The Bongos offer excellent contrast to the other drums in imitative passages.

5. These drums offer a welcome change from the Snare Drum.

THE CONGA DRUM

The Conga Drum, the bass of the Latin-American group of drums, is a one-headed drum of approximately 30 by 11 inches. Although the Conga Drum is available in several sizes, a composer, to be conservative, should restrict its use to one size.

The Conga Drum is played on a stand, between the knees, or slung over the shoulder on a strap. It is generally played with the palms and fingers. Using hand pressure on the head, as discussed under "Bongos," is a basic technique.

The Conga Drum.

BEATERS

Hands and fingers—a multitude of pitch and tonal varieties can be achieved by striking the drum in various places with the fingers and different parts of the hand.

Other—all kinds of beaters can be used.

DISTINCTIVE FEATURES

1. The rhythmic patterns played on the Conga Drum are generally less complex than those of the Bongos.

2. High and low pitches can be obtained by striking near the edge (for the high pitch) and in the center (for the low). This makes the need for two sizes of drums less urgent. Like the notation for playing the Cymbals on the edge and on the bell, the notation for the high-low on the Conga is best handled by using the x-headed note to show the high pitch. (See Ex. 7.4.)

3. The Conga Drum has uses far exceeding those practiced in Latin-American popular music.

THE TIMBALES

Timbales[2] are Latin-American instruments of rather recent origin. They come attached in pairs, single-headed drums without snares, with heads set on metal shells approximately 6 inches in depth. The high drum is approximately 13 inches in diameter, the low drum 14 inches. Fastened to a stand and generally played with Timbale sticks, these drums may also be played with the hands and fingers. Although these are considered drums of indefinite pitch, the heads of the drums may be tensioned to vary in pitch from a perfect fourth to a perfect fifth as desired. (This intervallic relationship between the two drums is usually determined by the preference of the performer.)

Like Bongos, the Timbales are capable of many sounds. Typical techniques include playing at the edge of the drum, center of the drum, on the shell, and rim shots. Because of the metal shells, their tone is more metallic and penetrating than the Tom-Toms.

Timbales are not too frequently found outside of Latin-American popular bands and percussion ensembles, but they offer the possibility of much wider use. In the Latin-American popular music, they sound their best when played ad lib.

The Timbales.

[2]*Timbales* in French scores refer to Timpani.

BEATERS

Timbale sticks—thin wooden dowel-like sticks, somewhat lighter than Snare Drum sticks, are the traditional sticks used in playing the Timbales.

The Maraca stick—this hollow stick filled with shot may be used on the Timbales (as well as on other drums) for a special effect, but the sticks are quite fragile and should be used with restraint.

Other—Timpani and Marimba mallets may be used for tonal variety. Fingers may also be used.

DISTINCTIVE FEATURES

1. The Timbales are an excellent variant for other drums, particularly the Tom-Toms.

2. They may be used antiphonally with the Bongos, Tom-Toms, and other high-low pairs of percussion instruments.

3. When used in typical Latin-American tradition, a notation problem arises because of the several tone variants possible on each drum. (For a recommended notation see Exs. 7.36, 7.37, and 7.38.)

4. Although the pitch is not particularly focused, the Timbales may be used as a poor substitute for the very rare Piccolo Timpani, but they are hand tuned with a key and therefore not readily adjustable.

THE COWBELL

Cowbells (called Cencerros in Latin-American circles) are made by manufacturers of percussion instruments in eight or more sizes. To be on the conservative side, the composer should probably specify "small," "medium," or "large," being reasonably assured that these sizes will be available.

Composers usually regard the Cowbell as an instrument of indefinite pitch. In Latin-American rhythms, the Cowbell generally maintains a one- or two-measure pattern, changing only at the end of definite sections. It can, however, play a "floating" part in which it constantly creates new rhythmic patterns to add color and contrast. Latin-American

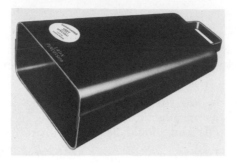

The Cowbell.

dances have definite rhythms assigned to the Cowbell. Otherwise, use the Cowbells like Cymbals, for color and accent.

Some rental houses have sets of Cowbells tuned to definite pitches. Since each set is different, it is not possible to be too specific. A composer should write for tuned Cowbells only when he is certain that they are available. Very few percussionists own tuned sets.

BEATERS

Snare Drum sticks—the most commonly-used beater. The butt is usually used.

Other—clave, mallets of steel, rubber, plastic, and other materials may likewise be used. The quality of tone produced can be easily imagined if no opportunity exists to hear these sounds.

DISTINCTIVE FEATURES

1. The Cowbell is traditionally struck in two places: on the top and on the lip. The difference between the two sounds is similar to the difference between playing on the bell and at the edge of a Suspended Cymbal, although the quality on the Cowbell is more bell-like and less sustained in both instances. The x-headed notes may be used for playing "on the top."

2. If the composer wants a muffled effect, he can specify "muted," or "semi-muted." Combinations of striking on the top or lip with the various muffling effects can give an impressively colored rhythmic pattern. (See Ex. 7.29.)

3. When using multiple sizes of Cowbells, even greater variety is possible.

4. A series of Cowbells may be arranged on a table and struck with

sticks in each hand. The Cowbells will be somewhat muffled in this case. Both jazz and orchestral drummers often use Cowbell holders.

5. In Latin-American music, the Cowbell is usually held in the hand. Brazilian popular music uses two attached Cowbells tuned to the interval of a third. This set is called an *Agogo*.

THE CLAVES

The Claves, another of the Latin-American group of percussion instruments, are two round pieces of hard wood, approximately 1 inch in diameter by 6 inches long. One Clave is held in the left hand, cupped to make a resonating chamber, and struck sharply by the Clave held in the right hand.

In their native Latin-American setting, the Claves generally play a repeated two-measure pattern to serve as the foundation for the various surrounding rhythms.

The Claves.

DISTINCTIVE FEATURES

1. As might be expected, the use of the Claves is primarily limited to the popular music of Latin-America. (Refer to the Latin-American rhythm books listed in the Appendix.)

2. Limit the writing for the Claves to basic rhythmic patterns. Rolls cannot be executed.

3. Isolated notes can add a brilliant touch of color to a staccato chord at any dynamic level.

4. Use Claves antiphonally with other percussive sounds.

THE MARACAS

The Maracas (also Sonajas), usually played in pairs (one in each hand), are gourds filled with seed, pebbles, or shot and attached to a handle. (Commercial versions also use wood and plastic rather than gourd.) Maracas, for the most part, have been imported from the Latin-American countries, but they are sold by most percussion manufacturers today. Sizes range from about 7 inches overall length to 12 inches. The smaller ones will normally have smaller shot (or seed) and have therefore a much more delicate sound. The larger ones are quite bold sounding. The average size is approximately 10 inches, with the ball being about 3 1/2 to 4 inches in diameter.

The Maracas.

DISTINCTIVE FEATURES

1. In the Latin-American popular music, Maracas usually play repeated eighth-note patterns or a simple two-measure pattern.

2. The use of Maracas should not be limited to typical Latin-American music. They can be used for other rather complex patterns.

3. The smaller Maracas are better for more delicate sounds, the larger for bolder and more penetrating sounds. Specify: "small," "medium," or "large."

4. The composer as well as the percussionist should know the following method of playing the Maracas: Hold the Maracas horizontally in each hand and tap on the top of the Maracas with the forefinger of each hand. This is especially good for soft passages, and it avoids

the grace note effect which occurs when the Maracas are held upright and are shaken. (Holding the Maracas horizontally and giving them a shallow, quick, downward movement gives a similar effect.) A passage written pianissimo will probably be played in one of the above manners.

5. Striking a suspended Maraca with Marimba mallets also produces a delicate sound.

6. Very fast rhythmic patterns can be executed by striking the Maracas against the knees.

7. The roll is effective on the Maracas. It may sound indefinitely and can be loud or soft.

8. A special kind of one-Maraca roll, with the Maraca held ball down (or ball up) and rotated, is possible. This is less intense than the two-Maraca roll. Specify: "one Maraca—ball down."

9. Maracas can be muted with the hand.

10. Composers can use Maracas in the same way they use other percussion instruments of indefinite pitch: to maintain a constant rhythmic background, to add color to held notes or trills, to add accent to isolated chords or rhythmic patterns, to contrast the sound of other percussion instruments, and to serve in a solo capacity.

THE GUIRO

The Guiro (Scraper, Scratcher, or Gourd) is traditionally a long bottle-type gourd[3] with a serrated side. It is scraped with a to-and-fro motion with a small wooden stick or other scratcher.

DISTINCTIVE FEATURES

1. Although used predominantly in Latin-American popular music, the Guiro produces a subtle sound that can be obtained on none of the other instruments. When played with a stiff wire, it approaches the sound of the Ratchet, but can be most effective in soft passages played with a small wooden stick. (A chopstick is often used.)

[3]The Guiro is also, but less frequently, made from a cow's horn.

The Guiro.

2. Although single sounds are impossible (unless one were to strike the gourd with the stick), a note of short duration sounds like a short roll, similar to the press roll on the Snare Drum. (It is not necessary to indicate these short notes as roll.)

3. The Guiro may be used as a variant for the membrane or wooden instruments. For variety, use it as a substitute for ornamented Snare Drum strokes, the short roll, and the stir with wire brushes.

THE RECO-RECO

The Reco-Reco (Reso-Reso) is a rasper, possibly of Brazilian origin. It is a long, hollow, serrated wooden or bamboo tube, played by drawing a small stick (or a wire brush for softer sounds) across the notches on the tube. The sound produced resembles that of the Guiro.

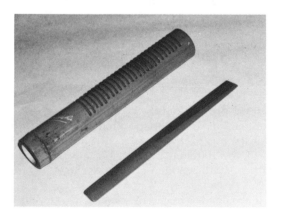

The Reco-Reco.

DISTINCTIVE FEATURES

1. The Reco-Reco plays patterns similar to both the Maracas and the Guiro in popular Latin-American music.

2. Refer to *Distinctive Features*, under the Maracas and the Guiro for other suggestions.

3. The Reco-Reco is an instrument rarely found in the percussion collection of non-Latin-American organizations.

THE CHOCALLO

The shakers traditionally form a part of all Latin-American percussion instruments. The Chocallo[4] is a long, fat *metal* tube filled with beads or shot. It is held in the hand and moved to and fro with a gentle rolling motion. Although the sound is similar to that of the Maraca, it is more metallic, as might be expected.

DISTINCTIVE FEATURES

1. In Latin-American popular music the Chocallo, as well as the Kameso, plays patterns similar to the Maracas.

2. Simple rhythmic patterns or rolls are possible on the Chocallo.

3. An imaginative mind might devise other uses for this instrument compatible with contemporary thinking in serious music.

The Chocallo.

[4]The Chocallo is also called (or spelled) Chocalho, Xocalho, Chocolo, Xucalho, Tubos, Metal "Tubo" Shaker, and Metal Tuba(!).

THE KAMESO

The Kameso (Kamesa or Camesa), similar in construction to the Chocallo, is a hollow tube of *wood* filled with shot or seed.

The Kameso is played in the same manner as the Chocallo, and the sound produced is similar, though less metallic.

The Kameso.

DISTINCTIVE FEATURES

See *Distinctive Features* under "Chocallo."

THE CABAZA

The Cabaza (Cabasa, Cabaça, and Casaba)[5] is another type of shaker: a large Maraca-like gourd covered with several loose strands of beads. The Cabaza is held with the handle in one hand with the gourd resting in the other. A rattling or swishing sound is created by the beads sliding across the serrated surface of the gourd. A performer may produce other sounds by such techniques as slapping the gourd or striking the beads with the fingers. (Some Cabazas do not have handles.)

The Cabazo.

[5]A serrated Cabaza is sometimes called an "Afoche."

DISTINCTIVE FEATURES

1. The typical rhythmic patterns often used are similar to those of the Maracas.

2. The Cabaza is another instrument rarely found outside of the Latin-American bands.

3. Again, this instrument offers possibilities for sensitive and creative writing in more contemporary styles. Arthur Cohn has written for a suspended "Cabaça" struck with small felt beaters in his *Quotations for Orchestra* (Mills Music, Inc.).

THE TAMBORIM

The Tamborim (not to be confused with Tamborin or Tambourine) is a small drum similar to a small Tambourine without jingles, or sometimes it is made in the shape of a shallow square box. It is held in the left hand and struck with a thin stick. Like the Pandeiro (see page 88) pressing the third finger of the left hand on the inside of the head produces varying pitches.

The Tamborim.

DISTINCTIVE FEATURES

·1. In Latin-American popular music the Tamborim plays simple two-bar riffs. The open versus hand-muted effect may be notated with the symbols 0 and +. (See Ex. 7.30)

2. Although the Tamborim is a very rare instrument outside of Latin-American bands, it could well serve for still another sound in the infinite collection of drum sounds which vary from extremely high to extremely low.

THE PANDEIRO

The Pandeiro (also Pandero) is an instrument almost identical to a Tambourine but with fewer jingles. It is basically a drum held in the left hand and played with the fingers, thumb, and heel of the right hand. Not so commonly found in the United States, even in Latin-American groups, it has still not found its way into more serious music. Many different sounds can be produced by striking the Pandeiro in various places on the head with fingers, thumb, or heel of the right hand, and by a pressure exerted on the back of the head by the third finger of the left hand.

The Pandeiro.

DISTINCTIVE FEATURES

1. In Latin-American popular music the Pandeiro plays patterns similar to the Bongos and Quica. (See below.)

2. Although orchestras or bands do not generally use this instrument, it offers percussive sounds which vary from other instruments. Its notation is similar to that of the Tamborim. (See Ex. 7.30.)

THE QUICA

The Quica (also Cuica and Puita) is a rare instrument, even in the Latin-American groups, and has achieved little or no recognition in symphonic or chamber music. Yet it is an intriguing instrument capable of a wide range of expression. Usually about the size of a deep Bongo, it is a single-headed drum with a small pole whose end is embedded in the inside center of the head. This pole is stroked with a damp cloth to produce the characteristic Quica sound. The Quica is normally kept in playing position by a strap similar to a Saxophone strap. The left hand is used both to steady the instrument and to vary the pitch. Change in pitch is accomplished both by pressing the fingers of the left hand

The Quica.

against the head of the drum and by varying the pressure on the stroking cloth.

Although the Quica has an extensive range of approximately three octaves, the composer should treat it as an instrument of indefinite pitch and notate it like other percussion instruments with relative pitch differences.

DISTINCTIVE FEATURES

1. In Latin-American popular music the Quica plays rhythmic patterns similar to Maracas, Bongos, or the Conga Drum. Conventionally, it is notated at two pitch levels like the Bongos.

2. Although the instrument is extremely uncommon in serious music, it is a challenge to the composer looking for new percussive sounds.

THE JAWBONE

The Jawbone (or Quijada), now available commercially, is an instrument found in only about a third of the professional concert organizations and to a still lesser extent in colleges. The performer holds the Jawbone (jawbone of the ass) in one hand and strikes it with the other, allowing the loose teeth to rattle.

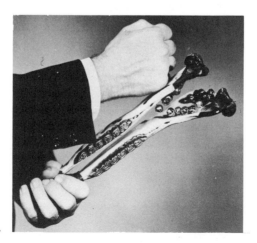

The Jawbone.

DISTINCTIVE FEATURES

1. The Jawbone plays the most simple part of all the Latin-American rhythm instruments. It is often used solely on the fourth beat of the measure, but is sometimes used to emphasize the syncopation of a rhythm such as appears in the Conga.

2. The Jawbone is used only for single notes.

Other Percussion
Instruments 6

The percussion instruments which are more generally used are discussed in detail in previous chapters. Although a complete listing of percussion instruments is impossible, this chapter lists others available in the United States, for sale or rental. Those listed here are classified under:

A. *Additional Percussion Instruments*
    The Drums; the Bells; the Wind Chimes; the Gongs (Tam-Tams); the Bird and Animal Calls; Horns; Whistles, and Effects; and Miscellaneous.

B. *Educational Rhythm Instruments*
    The Mallet Percussion Instruments; the Drums; the Metallic Instruments; and the Wooden and Gourd Instruments.

C. *Recorded Sounds*

The Educational Rhythm Instruments are included because of the significant work of Carl Orff and also because some of these instruments are professional in quality and have real artistic merit. Furthermore, some of the percussion instruments are available *only* from manufacturers of Educational Rhythm Instruments.

The composer of serious new music may find in the following lists of instruments a new and artistic challenge, but many of those listed are available only through rental shops.

A. Additional Percussion Instruments

The Drums

Bombi Drums
Bongale Drums
Clay Drums

Dumbeg[1]
Hebrew Love Drums
Lujon Drums

The Drums

Roc-o-rine
Steel Drums
Tabor Drums
Talking Drums
Thunder Drums

Tibetian Skull Drums
Turtle Drums
Voo-doo Drums
Water Drums

The Bells

Ankle Bells
Bell Lyra
Bicycle Bells
Call Bells
Carriage Bells
Ceremonial Bells
Corinthian Tea Bells
Death Toll Bells
Fight Bells
Fire Bells

Hand Bells
School Bells
Ship Bells
Song Bells
Steeple Tea Bells
Steeple Bells
Temple Bells
Wrist Bells
Yacht Bells

The Wind Chimes

Bamboo Chimes
Glass Chimes

Metal Chimes
Wood Chimes

The Gongs (Tam-Tams)

Balinese Gongs
Chinese Gongs
German Gongs
Indian Gongs

Italian Gongs
Japanese Hand Gongs
Javanese Gongs
Korean Gongs
Pakistan Gongs

The Bird and Animal Calls

Antelope Call
Baby Cry
Bear Growl
Bird Call Flute
Bird Whistle
Bob White Call
Canary Call
Cow Moo
Cricket Imitation
Crow Call
Cuckoo Call
Curlew Call
Deer Call
Dog Bark
Dove Call

Duck Quack
Elk Call
Frog Croaker
Goose Call
Hen Cackle
Jaybird Call
Lark Call
Lion Roar
Nightingale Call
Peacock Call
Ployer Call
Raccoon Death Cry
Rooster Call
Skylark Call
Snipe Call

[1]Also called Derabucca, Derbaki, Miriam Drum, Darbuka, Dumbecki, Tabla, and Greek Drum.

The Bird and Animal Calls

Squirrel Call

Tiger Roar

Turkey Call

Warbler Call

Widgeon Bird Warbler

Wounded Rabbit Cry

Horns, Whistles, and Effects

Auto Horn

Bass Drum Jingle Muffler

Bicycle Horn

"Boing" Box

Buzz Rattles

Cannon Shot

Chains

Ching-Ring

Cyclone Whistle

Diesel Horn

Dinner Chimes

Fog Horn

Gear Machine

Horses' Hoofs

Interurban Whistle

Klaxon Horn

Marching Machine

Ocean Liner Horn

Pan Rattles

Pistol Shot

Police Whistle

Pop Gun

Siren

Song Whistle

Steam Boat Whistle (2 or 3 tone)

Steam Exhaust

Taxi Horn

Thunder Machine

Train Imitation

Train Whistle (2 or 3 tone)

Tugboat Whistle

Typewriter

Washboard

Wind Machine

Miscellaneous

Balypso

Bamboo Marimba[2]

Baschet Instruments[3]

Bass Marimba

Bock-a-da-bock Cymbals

Boobams

Buzz-imba

Clavitimbre (chromatic)

Cloud-Chamber Bowls[2]

Contra Bass Marimba

Diamond Marimba[2]

Dinner Chimes

Flexitone (approx. range: e^2-g^3)

Keyed Glockenspiel

Leather Maracas

Marimba Eroica[2]

Marimbula (Thumb Piano)

Metal Castanets

Metal Maracas

Pele Sticks

Sistrum

Spoils of War[2]

Vibra-slap

B.   Educational Rhythm Instruments

The Mallet Percussion Instruments

Bars, Sonant (v.s.)[4]

Bell-Blocks, Tuned

Bells, Chromatic Bar

Bells, Chromatic Swiss (v.s.)

---

[2]Harry Partch instruments.

[3]The new Baschet Instruments are discussed in *The Music Educators Journal,* Vol. 49, No. 4.

[4]The abbreviation "v.s." indicates that *various sizes* are available.

The Mallet Percussion Instruments

Bells, Diatonic (v.s.)
Bells, Diatonic Swiss Melody
    (v.s.)
Bells, Resonator (v.s.)
Bells, Song (v.s.)
Bells, Step (v.s.)
Bells, Tone Educator (25)
Glockenspiels (v.s.)

Marimbaphones (v.s.)
Marimbas (v.s.)
Pianos, Toy
Vibes (v.s.)
Xylophones (v.s.)
Xylophone-Metallophones (v.s.)

The Drums

Bass Drums (v.s.)
Bongos (v.s.)
Conga Drums (v.s.)
Cylindrums (v.s.)
Drum Sets
Floor Drums
Hand Drums (w/without snares)
Oriental Drums
Redonda Drums (v.s.)
Reverbo Drums (v.s.)
Rhythm Drums (v.s.)
Single Hand Bongos
Snare Boy Drums

Snare Drums (v.s.)
Tenor Drums
Tiny Tymps (10", 12")
Tom-Toms, African
Tom-Toms, American-Indian (v.s.)
Tom-Toms, Chinese
Tom-Toms, Floor (v.s.)
Tom-Toms, Inca
Toy Drums
Tub Drums
Unibongo Drums

The Metallic Instruments

Bell, Liberty
Bells, Brass Indo
Bells, Camel (6)
Bells, Cluster
Bells, Cow (v.s.)
Bells, Diwali
Bells, Hand Rhythm
Bells, Multi-Cluster
Bells, Rhythm
Bells, Signal
Bells, Sleigh
Bells, Sleigh Wristlet
Bells, Sweet Meat
Bells, Swiss Hand
Bells, Tea
Bells, Temple
Bells, Turkish
Bells, Turkish Hand
Bells, Turkish Wrist
Bell Stick, Jingle

Castanets, Metal
Cymbals (v.s.)
Cymbals, Finger
Cymbals, Pat
Gong, Metal Tap
Gong, Nickel Plated
Gong, Plate
Gong, Rhythm
Jingle Clogs
Jingle Taps, Double
Jingle Taps, Triple
Shakers, Metal Rhythm (v.s.)
Tambourines, w/jingles (v.s.)
Tambourines, without
    jingles (v.s.)
Triangles (v.s.)
Tuning Bars (v.s.)

The Wooden and Gourd Instruments

Bones
Castanets, Finger

Castanets, Hand
Castanets, Spring

The Wooden and Gourd Instruments

Claves (v.s.)
Cocktail Shakers, small wood
Guiros (v.s.)
Maracas, Gourd (v.s.)
Maracas, Wood (v.s.)
Maraca Tube, Spanish
Rhythm Sticks
Spoons, Musical (plastic)

Tap-A-Taps (Pat-a-Cakes)
Temple Blocks (5)
Tick Tock Blocks
Tone Blocks, Chino (v.s.)
Tone Block, Claves
Tone Blocks, Guiro
Tuned Logs
Wood Blocks (v.s.)
Wood Blocks, Two-Tone

C. Recorded Sounds

Practically any sound desired is available on record or tape. Suppliers of these special sounds are listed under "Books and Recordings for Further Study." Catalogs are generally available on request.

Notation and Scoring

Special Characteristics
of Percussion Notation   **7**

Part I dealt primarily with the specifics of the various percussion instruments: ranges, transpositions, beaters, physical properties, methods of setting the instruments into vibration, and the distinctive features of each instrument. Part II deals with the problems of notation and scoring for percussion. Some problems of notation, however, are discussed and illustrated under the individual instruments in Part I.

THE STAFF

The mallet percussion instruments are traditionally written on a five-line staff using the G or F clefs. But composers have written instruments of indefinite pitch on one-line staffs, two-line staffs, five-line staffs, and have used a variety of contrived clef signs in addition to the G and F clefs.

The use of the one-line percussion staff probably resulted from using manuscript paper with printed instrumentation (with one-line percussion staffs)—usually a poor choice since few scores conform to any standard layout. It is generally better to use a plain style of manuscript paper with a sufficient number of staffs. Fortunately, this forces a composer to use the traditional five-line staff for *all* percussion instruments, a staff where instruments can be notated on assigned lines or spaces. This staff adapts particularly well to the approximate pitch movement so characteristic of such instruments as the Tom-Toms, Bongos, Timbales, and Temple Blocks.

Much as one might wish to assign a line or a space *permanently* to one instrument, it is not practical. Instrument assignment must often vary both from one score to another, and from one percussion part to another. (Far more percussion instruments are available than there are lines and spaces!) Nevertheless, it is possible to be reasonably consistent so far as the Snare Drum and Bass Drum are concerned. A few general suggestions can be made, but these are not binding and inflexible rules:

1. Write the membrane instruments on the spaces and the metallic, wooden, and gourd instruments on the lines. One possibility is shown below.

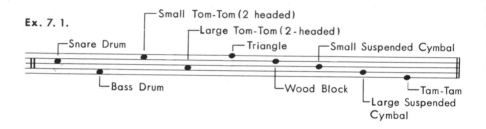

Ex. 7. 1.

(Unless a single staff is assigned to two percussionists, turn the stems down for all note heads above the second space and up for those below the third line.)

The five lines are also convenient to use for the five Temple Blocks; but, if possible, avoid writing two different instruments on the same line or space. It is possible, however, to use the fourth space for a small Tom-Tom in Percussion I and also for a high Bongo in Percussion II. Such duplications may be acceptable if unavoidable. (See Ex. 8.1.)

2. As nearly as possible, assign the higher-pitched instruments to the higher lines and spaces and the lower-pitched instruments to the lower lines and spaces.

3. Once an assignment is made, adhere to this plan throughout the composition.

4. For clarity and further reinforcement, where necessary, write the name of the instrument (or its abbreviation) at each entrance.

5. Leger lines may be used to accommodate more instruments or for better spacing to facilitate reading.

45854

THE CLEF

The mallet percussion instruments and the Timpani use the appropriate treble or bass clefs. There is no apparent reason to use the G or the F clefs for the percussion instruments of indefinite pitch. The use of the

neutral clef,  recommended by Donato, Fennell, Read,

and others, appears to be the best choice. Although its *raison d'être* is primarily esthetic, it does offer a way of cancelling the treble or bass clef signs when a percussionist changes from a *pitched* to an *unpitched* instrument.

Ex. 7. 2.

THE NOTE HEADS

The traditional note heads are recommended for notating all percussion instruments. A five-line staff generally eliminates the need to use symbols identified with certain instruments: symbols such as the x-headed note (♩), the diamond-headed note (♢), the square-headed note (◻), the triangle-headed note (◁), and such combinations (⊗) which attempt to show accurate duration. Most of these symbols are difficult to write with a music-writing pen.) A limited use of the x-headed note, and possibly other shapes, is justifiable when an instrument is set in vibration by some nontypical means.

 Normally the Snare Drum is played on the head with sticks, but it may also be played on the rim or shell; and the rim shot is a particular sound which must be clearly specified. Also, the Snare Drum can be played with wire brushes in various ways: single strokes, two-brush rolls, and the "stir."

 The Suspended Cymbal can be struck on the edge, on the bow, or on the bell, and can be set in vibration by other means such as drawing a Triangle beater across the top of the Cymbal. Most of the Latin-American instruments present similar notation problems, particularly the Bongos, the Conga Drum, and the Timbales. Although no binding rules of notation can be devised to cover all situations which might arise, some clarification is possible:

1. When various ways of setting the instrument into vibration occur in close succession, in single notes or short patterns, use the x-headed note for the nontypical stroke and describe the effect.

Ex. 7. 3.

Ex. 7. 4.

2. The use of wire brushes on the Snare Drum, with their various possibilities, presents some problems; but these can be solved in like manner.

Ex. 7. 5.

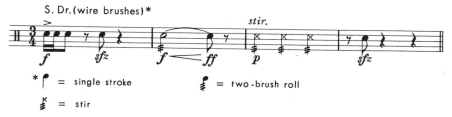

3. The use of a different kind of beater in each hand can be notated by use of the x-headed note.

Ex. 7. 6.

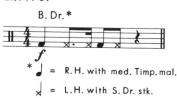

4. But use regular note heads when possible.

Ex. 7. 7.

Ex. 7. 8.

THE RIM SHOT

The rim shot, explained under the Snare Drum in Part I, is noted in the following way:

Ex. 7. 9.

THE UNMEASURED ROLL ON A SINGLE TONE

Although two ways have traditionally been used to notate an un-measured roll on one pitch, Ex. 7.10a is recommended.

Ex. 7. 10a.

Ex. 7. 10b.

All *mallet* percussion instruments *must* use the notation shown in Ex. 7.10a. To do otherwise would be a contradictory use of the sign (tr 〰〰) used for trills in mallet percussion as well as other melodic instruments.[1] It is therefore recommended that *all* percussion instruments (definite-pitched and indefinite-pitched) use the notation shown in Ex. 7.10a for the unmeasured roll.

Some mallet percussion performers roll each tone unless otherwise instructed. (This is their means of sustaining a tone—particularly on the Xylophone and Marimba.) But to avoid having rolls on single tones where none are intended, the warning "not to be rolled unless indicated" should be included. This warning is necessary only for the Xylophone and Marimba. If the roll technique is wanted, notate it as follows:

Ex. 7. 11.

Ties[2] should be used to connect notes in a continuous roll (Ex. 7.10a); otherwise there may be some separation between notes. A passage notated as in Ex. 7.12a might well be performed as in Ex. 7.12b.

Ex. 7. 12a.

[1] The Timpani have traditionally used the notation in Ex. 7.10b in spite of this ambiguity. Ex. 7.10a, however, is recommended for the unmeasured roll even for the Timpani.

[2] Some composers prefer to use the "broken" tie, reasoning that the tie does not accurately notate a continual reiterated note on the same pitch. The broken tie

$\left(\stackrel{....}{\overset{\rho \cdot}{} | \overset{\rho \cdot}{}}\right)$ may be used if one feels strongly about it.

Ex. 7. 12b.

Rolls on Cymbals, Tam-Tams, and other percussion instruments are notated as in Ex. 7.10a, except that the neutral clef sign and the appropriate line or space is used.

A special short, slide roll is possible on the Hand Cymbals. Notate as follows:

Ex. 7. 13a.   **Ex. 7. 13b.**

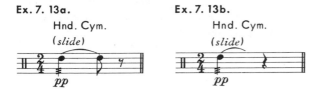

Ex. 7.13a indicates a specific duration. Ex. 7.13b indicates that the slide roll is brief, but the vibration lingers and gradually fades out.

Since the notes in Ex. 7.10a are tied it is unlikely, even in a slow tempo, that this example would be performed as measured thirty-second notes; however, to avoid this ambiguity, include the word "unmeasured."

Ex. 7. 14.

THE MEASURED ROLL

The abbreviation for the measured roll is best preceded by one unit correctly written out.

Ex. 7. 15.

THE UNMEASURED ROLL ON TWO TONES

An unmeasured roll on two tones is notated as follows:

Ex. 7. 16.

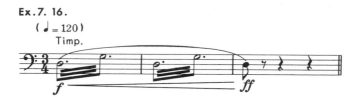

But, again, in a slow tempo include the word "unmeasured."

In MPI writing, an excusable exception to the agreement between performance and notational procedure occurs when the composer wants a roll between two tones in two-part writing.

Ex. 7. 17.

Obviously, a rapid reiteration between the two vertically aligned tones is wanted here. To notate this correctly is possible, but difficult to read, even for the simple example shown above.

ORNAMENTED NOTES

Ornamented notes constitute a significant part of the expressive vocabulary of Snare Drum writing and, to a lesser extent, the other percussion instruments. Grace notes are used primarily for the purpose of accent and for broadening a tone. In all instances these grace notes come *before* the beat and are not played as loudly as the main note which they ornament.

The degree to which these grace notes are moved closer to the note which they ornament ("closed") or farther from the primary note ("open") is determined by the performer. The composer can generally expect the "closed" effect in symphonic music.

The most common ornamentations are shown in the following chart.

Ex. 7. 18.

Notation	Number of grace notes	Name
♪ ♩	one	flam
♫ ♩	two	three-stroke ruff
♬ ♩	three	four-stroke ruff

If the composer wants more articulation on the grace note and volume approximately equal to the ornamented note, he should consider using exact metrical notation.

Ex. 7. 19.

(♩ = 120)

Percussionists often use a rebounding stroke (♬♩ or ♬♩)
(LLLR   LLLLR)

to interpret the ruff, but the grace notes are not a controlled and specific number in this instance. A combination of consecutive multibounce strokes is also used by some percussionists to produce a more "saturated" (closed) roll. William J. Schinstine[3] and Maurice D. Taylor[4] have used this technique (along with a specific notation) to bring the beginning drummer to a point where he can play a good, usable roll much quicker than he can by using the double-stroke technique.

Although there appears to have been no use of multibounce *notation* beyond its use as a training device (except for H. Owen Reed's *The Turning Mind*), the difference in sound between the rudimental and multibounce roll seems to justify its use by the serious composer. But it could be argued that such a fine point might better be left to the discretion of the percussionist. If this notation *is* used, however, it should be defined. Example 7.20 explains the technique of the multibounce roll and shows its notation.

[3]See William J. Schinstine, "Multiple Bounce Roll Notation," *Percussive Notes*, Vol. 4, No. 3, Feb. 1966, p. ii; and The Editors, "A Notation for Double and Multiple Bounce Strokes," *Percussive Notes*, Vol. 3, No. 4, May 1965, p. 9.
[4]Maurice D. Taylor, *Band Fundamentals in Easy Steps*, (New York: Mills Music, Inc., 1960).

Ex. 7. 20 Roll notation for drums (Timpani excluded*)

Notation	Name	Effect	Sticking
	Multibounce or Concert roll	more saturation than traditional roll	variable number of multibounces on each stroke: LLLRRR or LLLLRRRR
	Traditional, Rudimental, or Parade roll	less saturation than multibounce roll	a double bounce LLRR
	also a multibounce called <u>Press</u> or <u>Crush roll</u>	maximum saturation effect due to short duration	variable number of multibounces on each stroke (note) . . . one-stick press: LLLL or RRRR or two-stick press: LLLL RRRR

* The timpanist and mallet percussionist use the alternating stroke roll (LRLR) exclusively. Percussionists also use this stroke on any drum when <u>mallets</u> are used.

A similar extension of the grace note ornamentation would be notated 𝄽, preferably with the tie. One stick would rebound three or more times before the other articulated the primary note.

THE HALF TIE AND TONE DECAY

The half ties used in Ex. 7.21 indicate that the Cymbal should not be damped. This symbol has obvious advantages over a long series of tied notes. The direction "let vib." (or "l.v.") is sometimes included, but the half-tie notation should suffice.[5] (The use of the word "damp," while not essential, is probably best included here as a precaution.)

Ex. 7. 21.

[5] The half tie may be similarly used for any sustaining percussion instrument.

Notate specific durations the same as for nonpercussion instruments. Each percussion instrument has a varying amount of time for tone decay. The composer should be cognizant of these durations and notate his percussion parts to indicate accurately whether or not the tone is to be damped or allowed to vibrate. This is particularly essential for instruments such as the Tam-Tam, the Cymbal, and some MPI, less essential for the Timpani and the Bass Drum, and rather unessential for the Snare Drum and Wood Block. But an effort should always be made to represent accurately the desired sound (Ex. 7.31). When symbols become inadequate, one should state in precise English the effects desired.

THE TIMPANO GLISSANDO

The extremely effective Timpano glissando has not only been greatly used, but greatly abused. Although both the upward and the downward glissandos are possible, the upward glissando is better.

Ex. 7. 22.

Notice in Example 7.22 that the entire passage is played on the 25-inch Timpano. (Remember to consider the range.) Notice, too, that the glissando begins immediately on beat one in the first measure, but does not begin until the last eighth note in measure four. The third and final glissando is obtained by a single loud stroke. The tone will continue sufficiently long for the glissando to be made. The final **F** (notated as a grace note) will sound quite distinct without being restruck or rolled. A normal-sized note head on **F** would probably have implied that this note should be restruck. This again illustrates the need for precise notation.

CONFORMITY TO MELODIC WRITING

The mallet percussion instruments present few problems regarding notation. The notational characteristics of these instruments have generally paralleled the development of other melodic instruments and have become more or less standardized. Notational procedures for the percussion instruments of indefinite pitch, however, have not kept pace with practice.

Today's percussionist is a musician of high artistic ability who rightfully expects sensitive and accurate percussion writing. All of the subtleties of phrasing, dynamics, and rhythmic notation (consistently applied to brass, woodwind, and strings) should be a resolute part of percussion writing.

Although some disagreement exists (even among professional percussionists) concerning the extent to go in paralleling percussion notation with that of the melodic instruments, it seems evident that a close correlation is desirable. For example, if the Trumpets are playing a passage, such as in Ex. 7.23, it is better to use the same rhythmical notation for the Snare Drum.

Ex. 7. 23.

Whether or not the percussionist can actually produce an audible difference between eighth notes and quarter notes is irrelevant. The esthetic and psychological factors alone justify this conformity. And if the first measure were notated in quarter notes for Trumpets, the Snare Drum should be notated in quarter notes.

The complexities of twentieth-century rhythms create the need for a revision of the old method of using rests to approximate the short tone duration of instruments such as the Snare Drum. There is no apparent reason that the indefinite-pitched percussion instruments should not use notation which is easier to read and which, in most instances, parallels that of other instrumental notation.

Although we may disagree over the time it takes a tone to decay in a given instance, we can hardly dispute the fact that Ex. 7.24a is somewhat easier to read than Ex. 7.24b. And this is a very simple passage!

Ex 7. 24a

Ex. 7. 24b.

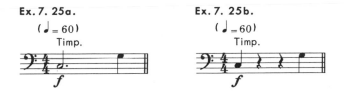

The notation of Ex. 7.24b should be followed only if the drummer is expected to damp on the rests. (This is not as essential on the Snare Drum as on instruments with greater sustaining abilities.) The percussion writing will be more intelligible to the conductor and performer if the composer follows the same procedures as for the wind or stringed instruments.

Rests should be observed in all instances by the proper damping technique except, perhaps, when writing for instruments with rapid tone decay. (See Ex. 7.31.) Example 7.25a should be performed differently from Ex. 7.25b.

Ex. 7. 25a.   Ex. 7. 25b.

As a result of careless notation in the past, MPI performers have often been forced to decide whether or not to roll a note. Modern-day percussionists look more and more to the composer for precise notation. If the composer anticipates ambiguity, he may wish to specify "not to be rolled unless indicated," or "don't roll."

Notice, too, that the slur is useful in percussion writing. In Ex. 7.26 the slur tells the performer to connect the two tones as smoothly as possible.

Ex. 7. 26.

The same principle applies to all percussion writing.

Ex. 7. 27.

HAND MUTED TONES

A tone with considerably less resonance may be produced on most of the percussion instruments by inhibiting vibration with the free hand. This technique is frequently used on the Suspended Cymbal to produce the Hi-Hat sound of open versus closed. This effect is best notated as follows:

Ex. 7. 28.

(Notice that the symbols are defined for the conductor and the performer. These symbols parallel those used to indicate open and stopped tones on the brass instruments.)

The Cowbell is often played in a similar manner.

Ex. 7. 29.

The two-bar riffs, characteristic of the writing for the Tamborim as well as many of the Latin-American instruments, are similarly notated.

Ex. 7. 30.

HAND DAMPING

Once sounded, the tones of a percussion instrument are generally not damped unless so indicated by the use of a rest. But sometimes there is the need to be more specific when writing for the definite-pitched percussion instruments, especially for those whose tones are more sustaining, such as the Timpani and the mallet percussion instruments—particularly the Vibe.

For special soloistic writing when exact rhythmical damping is desired, use a +-headed note (⨍ = **damp**) at the exact spot where the tone is to be damped.[6]

Ex. 7. 31.

THE DRUM SET NOTATION

In jazz, the drummer follows a rather simple chart which usually shows only the Snare Drum and Bass Drum part (sometimes a Cymbal) in simple rhythmic patterns. The drummer elaborates on these patterns dictated only by the arrangement and style. The measures which must coordinate with the ensemble are usually written out.

[6]For other examples of hand (or mallet) damped tones, see: Elliot Carter, *Recitative and Improvisation* for Four Kettledrums, (New York: Assoc. Music Publishers, Inc., 1960); Serge de Gastyne, *Menuet Très Antique* for Vibraharp Solo, (Alexandria, Va.: Fereol Publications, 1963); and Julius Wechter, *Play Vibes*, (New York: Henry Adler, Inc.), p. 16.

Example 7.32a shows a typical chart and Ex. 7.32b a possible realization. The following Identification Chart shows where each instrument will be notated on the staff. (See also Ex. 8.1.)

DRUM SET IDENTIFICATION CHART

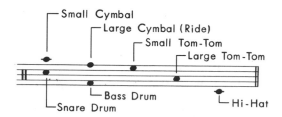

Ex. 7. 32a. (Chart)

Ex.7. 32b.(Possible realization)

For the jazz drummer such patterns are easier to improvise than to read; but Ex. 7.32b does illustrate the use of an exact notation for the Drum Set, should the need arise.

Example 7.33 notates a less complex Drum Set rhythm on one staff and, at the same time, illustrates notation for one of the basic patterns using wire brushes.

Ex.7. 33.

The left hand stirs quarter notes (see Ex. 7.5) while the right hand plays the rhythms indicated. (See "Distinctive Features" No. 11, under "Snare Drum.")

One example of a non-jazz use of the Drum Set follows in Ex. 7.34.

Ex.7. 34.

More complex writing should be notated on the grand staff.

In non-jazz usage, a composer might wish to use the Hi-Hat as a variant for a Suspended Cymbal. One possible notation for a pattern which uses both the sock and Suspended Cymbal effect follows:

Ex. 7. 35.

(See "Distinctive Features" No. 4 under "Hi-Hat.")

TIMBALE NOTATION

When Timbales are played in the Latin-American tradition, at least three sounds emerge to give these drums their special zest.

Ex. 7. 36.

Large Drum	Small Drum	Manner of striking

*The hand holding the stick strikes the head as the stick strikes both head and rim to combine a dull Tom-Tom sound with the rim shot.

Using the above notation, Ex. 7.37 illustrates a typical combination.

Ex. 7. 37.

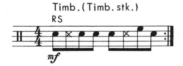

Timb.(Timb. stk.)

Perhaps equally important is playing on the shell with sticks (paille).

Ex. 7. 38.

Timb. (R.H. on shell)

(Explain *all* nontypical notation in the score and parts.)

The Full Score   **8**

The intent of the conscientious composer and the hope of the conductor are that the full score will be complete and intelligible in all details: instrument assignment, tempo indications, dynamics, phrasing, playing cues, and special instructions. Unfortunately, the percussion section too often does not receive the careful attention bestowed upon the other sections. But notation should be as clear for the percussion section as for the brass, woodwind, or string sections.

Conductors are grateful for scores which show on each page what percussion instrument is playing and which percussionist is responsible for its execution. In general, the score should include most of the information contained in the parts.[1]

Some details are characteristic of *parts* rather than the *score*: Whereas the performer needs advance warning for an instrument change (for example, "to Claves," or "to Xyl.") and instrument preparation (for example, "place Tamb. on head of 25-inch Timp."), the conductor needs only to see this information at the point of entrance (for example, "Claves," "Xyl," and "25-inch Timp.—with Tamb. placed on head"). Although the conductor is not particularly concerned with Timpani tuning indications, such instructions are not an encumbrance and should probably be included in the score. In fact, they serve as an asset when an inexperienced copyist must extract the parts, as is often the case.

Revisions in instrument distribution and responsibilities of percussion players will be made often *during the process of scoring*, but all problems must be solved and all responsibilities fixed before preparing the final ink score. The preparation and organization of an intelligent percussion score is difficult and perplexing, but *most* important.

[1]See "Characteristics of the Percussion Parts," in Chapter 9.

ORGANIZATION OF PLAYERS

The percussion is located on the score just below the brass and above the Harp and/or Piano, with the Timpani at the top of the percussion group. The number of staffs needed will depend upon the percussion requirements for each score, but one staff is usually assigned to each performer who may play several instruments.

The timpanist is treated somewhat as a prima donna and is generally assigned to play only the Timpani. In rare instances and when the need is sufficiently urgent, the composer may assign other percussion instruments to the Timpanist, but he *must* be allowed adequate time for tuning. (In the latter case his part would be labeled "Percussion I." Otherwise, it would be labeled "Timpani," with the next part becoming "Percussion I.")

There is a growing trend toward specialization among percussionists. The areas of specialization group themselves as follows: (a) Timpani, (b) Mallet Percussion Instruments, (c) Drums, and (d) Cymbals; but although percussionists tend to specialize, they can all freely interchange instruments and should be expected to do so when the need arises. Nevertheless, it is desirable to concentrate the mallet percussion instrument writing in one part. Likewise, since snare drumming requires considerable skill, passages for this instrument should usually be relegated to one performer. (This does not imply that it does not take considerable skill and experience to play artistically such instruments as the Cymbals and Bass Drum.)

A timpanist and three other percussionists may conservatively be used, but an excessive number of percussionists often jeopardizes performance possibilities. The demands of the music and the intent of the composer will dictate not only the number of Timpani but also other percussion requirements as well. The number of these instruments required and their use will in turn determine the number of performers. (Chapter 9 discusses this problem in more detail.)

LISTING OF INSTRUMENTS

Most scores today list on the instrumentation page only the percussion instruments to be used, along with the woodwind, brass, and strings. This listing should be expanded to include a Percussion Identification

Chart. Example 8.1 shows this chart and how *one* selection of percussion instruments might appear on this page.

Ex.8.1. Percussion identification chart.

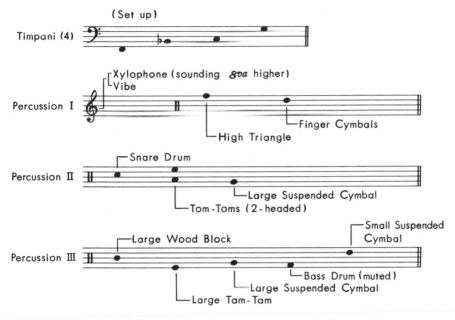

Other instructions or notational clarifications may be included here. A composer may even wish to suggest a particular arrangement of the instruments, an arrangement which would feature or project certain instruments, or would embody some aspects of spatial music.

Not only are the required number of performers shown in the above chart, but also the instrument distribution, the kinds and sizes of instruments used, instrument preparation, the line or space on the staff where each will be notated in the score and parts, and a note regarding the Xylophone transposition. (See also "The Staff," p. 99.)

After the page listing the instrumentation comes the first score page, showing complete listing of the instruments (not abbreviated) to be used. The exception to the customary listing on this page is the percussion section. If this listing is included before this, as recommended in Ex. 8.1, only the following is required:

Timpani
Percussion I
Percussion II
Percussion III

Therefore, on subsequent pages, use abbreviations as follows:

Timp.
Perc. I
Perc. II
Perc. III

(But see Chapter 9.)

SPECIAL NOTATION IN THE SCORE

The name or the abbreviation of the specific percussion instrument should be placed at each initial entrance and thereafter in parentheses, as a reminder to the conductor, on each subsequent page. If the Percussion Identification Chart calls for *only* a large Suspended Cymbal, use the abbreviation "Sus. Cym.," or even "Cym."; otherwise, specify size and type at each entry.

It is usually essential to indicate other pertinent information above the staff for each instrument: the manner of setting the instrument in vibration (if this is nontypical), muting or other instrument preparation, and kinds of beaters to be used. These indications are an integral part of the art of scoring, and they should be a part of the initial creative planning rather than a late and hurried appendage.

Since the timpanist is generally required to change the pitch of his Timpani during the performance, a composer must always allow sufficient time to make such pitch changes. This assumes that the composer, as well as the timpanist, is constantly aware of the sizes of the Timpani being used, as well as the range of each Timpano being tuned.

Timpani tuning instructions traditionally specify, for example, "change *G* to *A*." But if there happens to be both a high and a low *G* set up, some further instruction is required. The following method of indicating changes is therefore recommended on both the score and parts. It also has "eye appeal" to the timpanist.

Ex. 8. 2.

TRANSPOSITION IN CONCERT SCORES

A word of caution is needed here: In the concert (C) score, it is usually customary to write those instruments which transpose at the octave (or double octave) at their "written" pitches. This also applies to those mallet percussion instruments which transpose in this way. An instruction such as the following would be appropriate on the instrumentation page:

Concert Score. Instruments which transpose at the octave (or double octave) are notated at their written pitch.

Since writers have generally not agreed upon the transposition of some mallet percussion instruments, it is desirable to indicate their transposition on the instrumentation page as well as on the parts, regardless of the use of a *transposed* or *concert* score. (See Ex. 8.1.) *Always* include any information which makes for a clearer understanding of the score.

REDUCTION OF PERCUSSION REQUIREMENTS

Another problem concerns the reduction of percussion requirements in, for example, the second movement of a large work. The best solution here is to use the minimum number of players. A percussionist would prefer to "sit out" a movement—or an entire work—rather than count measures and play only a few notes. Always use the minimum number of performers, but also avoid creating the visual appearance of a game of musical chairs among the percussion performers. But such a reduction might require a new Identification Chart unless the original one satisfied the requirements for all movements.

The Percussion Parts   **9**

As the writing in the score must convey the composer's intent to the conductor, so too must the extracted parts convey his intent to the performer. Since a new work rarely receives sufficient rehearsal time, the composer must be particularly attentive to the preparation of a neat and accurate set of parts. Obtaining a performance or an award might depend upon the outcome of a preliminary reading. Many a new composition receives its first performance in a symposium where the first reading *is* the performance.

Under these circumstances, each percussionist must know precisely what he is to do and, preferably, what the other percussionists are to do. Assigning instrumental responsibilities to each percussionist not only assures a clear understanding of his performance responsibilities, but helps in the preparation and placement of the percussion instruments for a rehearsal or a performance.

TWO WAYS OF EXTRACTING PERCUSSION PARTS

In the extraction of the percussion parts from the full score, a composer has the choice of extracting each part separately (a part for Timpani, one for Percussion I, another for Percussion II, etc.) or writing the percussion parts in the form of a percussion score. In extracting parts in the form of the percussion score, the composer copies only one part—grouping all the percussion performers' parts together as they appear in the full score; but the Timpani part should generally be a separate one. Additional percussion parts are obtained by duplication.

The score form is better for modest percussion requirements since each performer can see what the other percussionists are playing; but if percussion requirements are too extensive, then the use of this form is not feasible. It limits the number of measures per page and may require a page turner for each percussionist—obviously impractical! To solve this problem, copy a separate part for each performer or employ some combination of the above two methods; for example, the Timpani alone, Percussion I alone, and Percussion II and III together. A "reduced" percussion score is another alternative. (See Ex. 9.1.)

Regardless of which method of score extraction the composer uses, he should include a Percussion Identification Chart at the top of the first page. If he adopts the percussion score plan, then this chart will appear the same as on the instrumentation page of the full score. (See Exs. 8.1 and 9.1.)

If he decides to extract each percussionist's part separately, then only the Percussion Identification Chart for this performer need be included. The beginning of page one for the Percussion I part, for example, might appear as shown on page 126.

Ex. 9.1.

Percussion Identification Chart

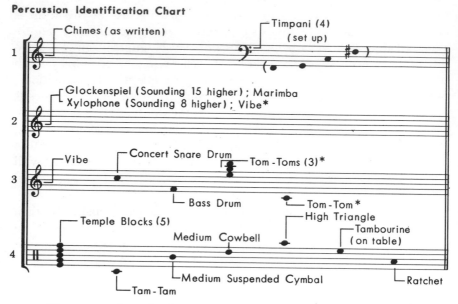

*If commercial two-headed Tom-Toms are not available, appropriate substitutions may be made for the three relative pitches.

†Only one each of the above instruments is required.

Suggested Arrangement

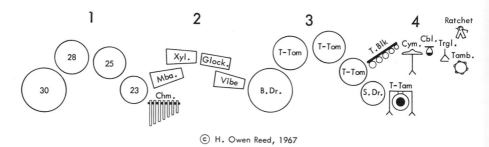

© H. Owen Reed, 1967

The Turning Mind

1. Introspection

H. Owen Reed

Ex. 9.2.

Percussion I

LA FIESTA MEXICANA

A Mexican Folksong Symphony

I. Prelude and Aztec Dance

Chimes,* Marimba*
Xylophone* ⎯⎯ Temple Blocks (1-4)

H. Owen Reed

Allegro maestoso (♩=50-60)

Chimes (solo)

etc.

*Marimba and Chimes sound as written. Xylohone sounds
an octave higher than written.

© 1964, Mills Music, Inc., N.Y.

Reprinted by permission of the publisher, Mills Music, Inc.

CHARACTERISTICS OF THE PERCUSSION PARTS

The percussion parts, like those of the other instruments, vary from the writing in the full score in several specific ways:

1. Consecutive measures of rest are grouped together and indicated as in Exs. 7.2 and 8.2.

2. When a performer has more than approximately ten measures of rest, a cue should be supplied. A prominent instrumental part should be used for this purpose and written in the appropriate clef, using the traditional small cue notes stemmed according to proper procedure. Using adequate cues is particularly essential for the timpanist, who must give his full attention to tuning. Using cues between percussion parts is also desirable unless the percussion score is used.

3. The name of the specific percussion instrument, or its abbreviation, should be placed at each initial entrance and thereafter in parentheses.

4. Instructions to change to another instrument, to tune, or to change beaters must appear immediately after the previous passage to forewarn the performer. (See Exs. 7.2 and 8.2.) These instructions may also be included in the score.

5. Pages are laid out in the traditional manner with odd-numbered pages to the right. Allow adequate time for page turning at the bottom of the odd-numbered pages. If no page turn is required on the initial page, it will be numbered page two and bound on the left side. If a page turn is needed on the initial page, it is considered page one and bound on the right side.

6. Since the percussionist will generally be farther from his music than other performers, a larger staff with larger notes is preferable for his part. Ten- or twelve-staff manuscript paper is best.

Other than the above six points, the percussion parts should correspond to the notation in the full score. Copy edit, copy, then proofread before duplicating. If one percussionist has to move from one principal instrument to another (for example, from Xylophone to Marimba), supply him with two copies of his part, one for each instrument.

For further help in music notation refer to Gardner Read, *Music Notation* (Boston: Allyn and Bacon, Inc., 1964), and Anthony Donato, *Preparing Music Manuscript* (Englewood Cliffs, New Jersey: Prentice-Hall, Inc., 1963).

Percussion as an Integral Part
of the Compositional Scheme   **10**

Whether one is writing for large symphonic groups or small chamber ensembles, the composer should decide at the beginning how many percussion instruments to use. Although you may think of percussion as an *adjunct* to harmony, rhythm, and melody, present-day requirements prescribe an *integral* approach where from the beginning the composer considers the total instrumentation (including percussion) in the creative process. The only limitations are those imposed by the availability and technical limitations of the percussion instruments and their performers.

DECIDING UPON THE INSTRUMENTATION

As a composer decides upon the choice of stringed, woodwind, or brass instruments to be used, so too does he decide upon the choice of percussion instruments. For a particular composition he may not need percussion: a string quartet, for example. Or he may wish to compose a work entirely dominated by percussion sounds: a composition for percussion ensemble. Usually his demands will be somewhere between these extremes.

Since composers vary in their approach to writing a score, it is impossible to prescribe a formula to fit every need. But a composer should at least have basic percussion requirements in mind before starting. Ideally, he will make a decision which will not need many changes, once the pencil copy of the score is completed.[1]

---

[1]The complexities of scoring for percussion make the intermediate process of the pencil score even more desirable. This is especially true when the demands for several players and many percussion instruments are severe.

One might proceed with the following basic structure for the percussion arrangement in writing the pencil score:

Timpani
Percussion I (mallet percussion instruments)
Percussion II (Snare Drums and other membrane instruments)
Percussion III (Bass Drum and accessorics)
Percussion IV (Cymbals and accessories)

No doubt the composer will find it necessary to deviate from this arrangement in the process of scoring, but any additional instruments or duplications can be appropriately assigned to the above performers, keeping in mind that the timpanist is generally not asked to participate. Percussionist III may need to play a chord on the Vibe while Percussionist I plays Xylophone; or perhaps Percussionist II may need to play Cymbals while Percussionist IV plays Tam-Tam. It is even likely that the composer will decide to add an additional performer (Percussionist V) to satisfy all of his needs. He can make these changes during the process of composition or scoring, *but before he makes the final ink copy of the score, he must think out a new and logical realignment and assignment of instruments.* (It is always advisable to leave one or more blank staffs on the pencil score, staffs which can be used for additional percussion requirements, or even for divisi strings.)

In summary, remember that it is essential to show the number of percussion players needed, which instruments each will be playing, and on which line or space each instrument will be notated.

MELODIC THINKING IN PERCUSSION WRITING

In the new music one finds an increasing use of "percussive" sounds by nonpercussive instruments. The snapping of the string of the Violin against the fingerboard and the Flute fluttertongue are two examples.

As the stringed and wind instruments are borrowing from the percussion sounds, so too are the percussion instruments borrowing from the melodic sounds. This melodic thinking has of course always been associated with the mallet percussion instruments, but recently there has been an increased awareness of the melodic (or simulated melodic) possibilities inherent in the percussion instruments of *indefinite* pitch.

Of those instruments discussed in Part I, only the following instruments are generally considered in the definite pitch category: Xylophone, Marimba, Vibe, Orchestra Bells, Chimes, Crotales, Pitched Gongs, and

Timpani. All others, with few exceptions, are classified as instruments of indefinite pitch.

It was previously noted that most of the instruments of indefinite pitch had a predominating tone which varied from a clear bell-like tone (as in the Cowbell) to a rather vague and almost indiscernible pitch (as in the Cymbal). Most of the instruments of indefinite pitch (being made in different sizes, or capable of producing different pitches according to striking techniques) can produce relative pitch differences— at least high and low, or high, medium, and low. Instruments such as the Temple Blocks and the One-headed Tom-Toms fall almost on the borderline between the definite and indefinite groups.

To further complicate classification of the indefinite-pitched instruments, such instruments as the Cowbells are sufficiently definite in pitch to be used as pitched instruments. Indeed, some composers have written for "tuned" Cowbells and have used Timbales to extend the upward range of the Timpani. While many of these are capable of producing definite pitches, it is generally advisable to think of them in terms of *indefinite* pitch or *relative* pitch. The latter suggests an extended role for these instruments.

Except for rare and perhaps precarious use on scalewise passages, the Timpani are generally limited to four-note motives. Music is almost always divisible into motives and submotives, and the Timpani have traditionally been used to state them in a solo capacity. In this way the Timpani have been used melodically. It only remains to treat the indefinite-pitched instruments in a similar fashion.

Whereas the Timpani can sound exact pitches in melodic writing, the instruments of indefinite pitch can usually only simulate pitch contour; but the latter have an uncanny way of absorbing pitches when doubled with instruments of definite pitch. They even seem to be definite-pitched when imitating or repeating a previously-stated motive by a pitched instrument. This is particularly true of such instruments as the Bongos, Timbales, and Temple Blocks.

This kind of thinking, in scoring for percussion, offers more possibilities for sensitive and integral writing for all of the percussion instru-

Ex. 10.1.   **Ex. 10.2.**

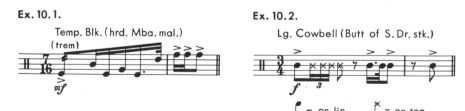

ments. The awareness of these relative pitch differences which occur between different instruments, between the same instrument in different sizes, or the same instrument struck in different places, makes it possible to write melodically for the indefinite-pitched percussion instruments.

PERCUSSION AS DECORATION

Although the above remarks suggest an extension of the use of percussion to incorporate more melodic writing, do not neglect the traditional use of percussion for decoration. (Review "Distinctive Features" of each instrument in Part I.) The decorative rather than the functional use of percussion involves the principle of doubling, but like all doubling, it should not be used to excess. Still, the addition of Orchestra Bells to a high woodwind or string melody, or the doubling of a poignant-muted brass chord with Vibe or Xylophone, can sound magical.

Although the limitations are governed only by one's imagination, a rule of thumb recommends the high-pitched percussive sounds with high-pitched melodies and chords and low-pitched percussive sounds with low-pitched melodies and chords.

Given the knowledge
concerning the availability of percussion instruments,
the general sizes in which they come,
the various beaters available,
the numerous techniques used for setting instruments into vibration,
the technical limitations on each, and
the notational techniques for accurate communication,

a composer is better equipped to approach the problems of scoring for percussion with renewed confidence that he will be more adequately prepared to write correctly for these instruments and will be confident that the percussionist will perform his music in the manner intended.

The composer is now urged to consult with professional percussionists and to experiment with the instruments in order to become better acquainted with their sounds and capabilities.

Books, Periodicals, and Recordings for Further Study

BOOKS AND PERIODICALS

Araújo, Alceu Maynard, *Folclore Nacional*, Vol. II. Sao Paulo: Ediçoes Melhoramentos, 1964.

Barnett, Wallace, *The Mallet Percussions and How to Use Them*. Chicago: J. C. Deagan, Inc., 1964.

Bartlett, Harry, *Guide to Teaching Percussion*. Dubuque: Wm. C. Brown, 1964.

Blades, James, *Orchestral Percussion Technique*. London: Oxford University Press, 1961.

Burns, Roy, *The Selection-Care-and Use of Cymbals in the Stage and Dance Band*. New York: Henry Adler, Inc., 1964.

Collins, Myron, and John Green, *Playing and Teaching Percussion Instruments*. Englewood Cliffs, N. J.: Prentice-Hall, Inc., 1962.

Denov, Sam, *The Art of Playing the Cymbals*. New York: Henry Adler, Inc., 1963.

Evans, Bob, *Authentic Bongo Rhythms*. New York: Henry Adler, Inc., 1960.
——— *Authentic Conga Rhythms*. New York: Henry Adler, Inc., 1960.

Firth, Vic, *Percussion Symposium*. New York: Carl Fischer, Inc., 1966.

Goldenberg, Morris, *Modern School for Snare Drum* (with a guide book for the artist percussionist). New York: Chappell & Co., 1955.

Kirby, Percival, *The Kettle Drums*. London: Oxford University Press, 1930.

Leach, Joel T., *Percussion Manual for Music Educators*. New York: Henry Adler, Inc., 1964.

Ludwig Drummer, a semi-annual publication. Chicago: The Ludwig Drum Company.

Magalhaes, Paulo Fernando (Paulinho), *Rhythms and Instruments of Brazil*. Translated by Roy Harte. Hollywood: D. G. Pub. Co., 1965.

Morales, Humberto, and Henry Adler, *Latin-American Rhythm Instruments and How to Play Them*. New York: Henry Adler, Inc., 1958.

Ortiz, Fernando, *Los Instrumentos de la Música Afrocubano*, Vols. I–V. Habana: Publicaciones de la Dirección de Cultura del Ministerio de Educación, 1952.

Payson, Al, and Jack McKenzie, *Music Educators, Guide to Percussion.* New York: Henry Adler, Inc., 1966.

Percussionist, a quarterly publication by the Percussive Arts Society, 1949 Dahlen Avenue, Terre Haute, Indiana, 47805.

Percussive Notes, a quarterly publication. 5085 Henderson Heights, Columbus, Ohio, 43221.

Peters, Gordon B., *Treatise on Percussion.* Masters Thesis, Eastman School of Music, 1062.

Price, Paul, *Triangle, Tambourine, and Castanets.* New York: Music for Percussion, 1955.

Shivas, Andrew A., *The Art of Timpanist and Drummer.* London: Dennis Dobson, 1957.

Spinney, Brad, *Encyclopedia of Percussion.* New York: American Federation of Musicians, Local 802. (Vols. A, B)

Spohn, Charles L., *The Percussionist.* Boston: Allyn and Bacon, Inc., 1967.

Taylor, Henry W., *The Art and Science of the Timpani.* London: John Baker, 1964.

Tilles, Bob, *Practical Percussion Studies.* New York: Henry Adler, Inc., 1962.

Torrebruno, Leonida, *Metodo per Strumenti a Percussione.* Milano: G. Ricordi & Co., 1960.

Wechter, Julius, *Play Vibes.* New York: Henry Adler, Inc., 1962.

White, Charles, *Drums Through the Ages.* Los Angeles: Sterling Press, 1960.

Wildman, Lewis, *Practical Understanding of the Percussion Section.* Boston: Bruce Humphries Publ., © 1964.

RECORDINGS

Adventures in Cacophony, Audiophile Records, Inc., Mono AP-37.

Echoes of the Storm, Audiophile Records, Inc., Mono AP-20.

Latin-American Rhythms, London Records, No. 155.

Latin Rhythms by Sam Ulano, Lane Recordings.

Recorded Sound Effects, Elektra Corporation.

Recordings of insects, bird songs, sounds of the sea, sounds of animals, etc., Children's Music Center, Inc.

Sound effects and background music (recorded on one quarter-inch tape and disc), Corelli-Jacobs.

Sound effects, ethnic recordings, records on jazz drumming, playing the Bongos, etc., Folkways Records.

Special sound effects and mood music (recorded on tape and disc), Thomas J. Valentino, Inc.

Spotlight on Percussion, Vox DL-180.

A recording by Jacques Lasry and Daniel Duzounoff, using the new Francois Baschet instruments is available from the Museum of Modern Art, 11 West 53rd Street, New York, N.Y., 10019 and will soon be released by Record and Tape Sales in New York.

Appendix 1:
Suggested Abbreviations

Listed below are suggested abbreviations for the more common percussion instruments. No abbreviations are given for some of the instruments with short names, nor are there abbreviations shown for some of the instruments of foreign origin, or for those which might be difficult to identify by use of abbreviations.

Abbreviations should be used only if:

a. the instrument has been identified *by full name* on the Percussion Identification Chart, and/or

b. the abbreviation could not represent one of the many other percussion instruments.

Antique Cymbals (Ant. Cym.)
Anvil (Anv.)
Bass Drum (B. Dr.)
Bell Plate (Bell Pl.)
Bongos (write out)
Brake Drum (Brk. Dr.)
Cabaza (Cabz.)
Castanets (Cast.)
Chimes (Chm.)
Chinese Tom-Tom (Chin. T-Tom)
Chocallo (Choc.)
Claves (Clav.)
Conga Drum (Cong. Dr.)
Cowbell (write out)
Crotales (write out)
Cymbal (Cym.)
Drum Set (Dr. Set)
Elephant Bells (Eleph. Bells)
Finger Cymbals (Fing. Cym.)
Flexitone (Flex.)
Guiro (write out)
Hand Cymbals (Hnd. Cym.)

Hi-Hat (H.H.)
Indian Drum (Ind. Dr.)
Log Drum (Log Dr.)
Kameso (Kam.)
Maracas (Mrcas.)
Marimba (Mbr.)
Orchestra Bells (O.B.)
Pandeiro (Pand.)
Parade Drum (Prd. Dr.)
Quica (write out)
Quijada (Quij.)
Ratchet (Ratch.)
Reco-Reco (R-R)
Sand Blocks (Sand Blk.)
Sizzle Cymbal (Siz. Cym.)
Slapstick (Slapstk.)
Sleigh Bells (Sl. Bells)
Snare Drum (S. Dr.)
Suspended Cymbal (Sus. Cym.)
Tamborim (write out)
Tambourine (write out)
Tam-Tam (T-Tam)

Temple Blocks (Temp. Blk.)
Tenor Drum (Ten. Dr.)
Timbales (Timb.)
Timpani (Timp.)
Tom-Tom (T-Tom)
Tone Block (Tone Blk.)
Triangle (Trgl.)

Tuned Gong (write out)
Vibe (write out)
Wood Block (Wd. Blk.)
Xylophone (Xyl.)

Other abbreviations

Small (Sm.)
Medium (Med.)
Large (Lg.)
High (IIgh.)
Low (write out)

Fan (write out)
Motor (mtr.)

Let vibrate (l.v.)
Measured (meas.)
Tremolo (trem.)
Vibrato (vib.)

Stick (stk.)
Mallet (mal.)
Beater (btr.)
Brushes (brsh.)
Brass (write out)
Cord (crd.)
Felt (flt.)
Hard (hrd.)
Plastic (plas.)
Rawhide (rhd.)
Rubber (rub.)
Soft (sft.)
Steel (stl.)
Wood (wd.)
Yarn (yn.)

Appendix 2:
Acknowledgments

The authors of *Scoring for Percussion* are particularly grateful for the cooperation given them by many professional percussionists, percussion manufacturers, percussion dealers, rental shops, recording companies, composers, colleagues, students, friends, and families.

Of particular value was the high return from questionnaires sent to many percussionists in both the college and professional areas. The following list gives recognition to those who were so cooperative in returning questionnaires, as well as others who have answered many questions and experimented with the material in this book.

June Albright, J. C. Deagan, Inc.
Hugh Allison, Drum City Enterprises, Inc.
Shirley Anderson, Percussion Instructor, Combs College of Music
John Baldwin, Percussion Instructor, Wisconsin State University, Oshkosh
John Beck, Timpanist, Rochester Philharmonic Orchestra and Instructor of Percussion, Eastman School of Music
Remo Belli, President, Remo, Inc.
John R. Bowen, Music Consultant, Torrance, California
Carroll Bratman, Carroll Musical Instrument Service
Mervin Britton, Assistant Professor of Percussion, Arizona State University
Larry Bunker, Percussionist, Los Angeles, California
Donald G. Canedy, Director of Education and Research, Rogers Drum Company
Bobby Christian, Percussionist, Composer and Arranger, Chicago, Illinois
Arthur Cohn, Author and Composer, New York, N.Y.
Arthur Cooper, Principal Percussionist, Detroit Symphony Orchestra
Richard A. Craft, President, Amrawco
Wallace E. DePue, Composer, Bowling Green State University
L. A. DiMuzio, Avedis Zildjian Company
Cloyd Duff, Timpanist, Cleveland Symphony Orchestra

Clare Fischer, Composer-arranger-pianist, Hollywood, California

George Frock, Assistant Professor of Music, University of Texas

Ruben Gonzalez, Cuban Singer and Conga Drum Player, New Orleans, Louisiana

Haskell W. Harr, Director of Education, Slingerland Drum Company

Roy Harte, President, Drum City, Hollywood, California

Erwin Honsa, Percussion Director, Morton East & West High Schools, Cicero, Illinois

Fred M. Jacobs, President, Corelli/Jacobs Film Music, Inc.

G. C. Jenkins, President, G. C. Jenkins Company

Jack Normain Kimmell, Composer-arranger-pianist, Grand Rapids, Michigan

Roy C. Knapp, Educational/Technical Director, Franks Drum Shop, Chicago, Illinois

Alan Laschiver, West Coast Drum Shop

Joseph Leavitt, Principal Percussionist, National Symphony Orchestra

Maxine Lefever, Percussion Instructor, Purdue University

Charles Lishon, Franks Drum Shop, Chicago, Illinois

Maurie Lishon, Franks Drum Shop, Chicago, Illinois

Rey M. Longyear, Associate Professor of Musicology, University of Kentucky

William F. Ludwig, Jr., Vice-president, Ludwig Drum Company

William H. Lyons, President, Lyons Band Instrument Company

Thomas McMillan, Percussionist and Instrumental Director, Pontiac, Michigan

Betty Masoner, Percussionist, Bemidji, Minnesota

Joe Morello, Percussionist and Clinician, Ludwig Drum Company

John Noonan, Percussionist, Normal, Illinois

Charles Owen, Principal Percussionist, Philadelphia Symphony Orchestra

Dean Pappas, Manager, Education Department, Carl Fischer, Inc.

Al Payson, Percussionist, Chicago Symphony Orchestra

Gordon Peters, Principal Percussionist, Chicago Symphony Orchestra; Percussion instruction, Northwestern University

Mitchell Peters, Principal Percussionist, Dallas Symphony Orchestra

Paul Price, Head of Percussion Department, Manhattan School of Music

James D. Salmon, Associate Professor of Percussion, University of Michigan

William J. Schinstine, Percussionist and Director of Music, Pottstown Senior High School, Pottstown, Pennsylvania

Dick Schory, Educational Director, Ludwig Drum Company

James Sewrey, Assistant Professor of Percussion and Principal Percussionist, Wichita Symphony Orchestra

Gary Sherman, Percussionist, Texas Technological College

Emil Sholle, Percussionist, Cleveland Symphony Orchestra

Hugh Soebbing, Instructor of Percussion, Quincy College

Phil Stanger, Percussion Instructor, Chicago, Illinois

Oscar Stover, Director of Bands, Northwestern State College (Oklahoma)

Maurice D. Taylor, Composer-Educator, Montrose, Pennsylvania
Harold J. Thompson, Percussionist, Boston Symphony Orchestra
Bob Tilles, Professor of Music, De Paul University; C.B.S. Chicago
Larry Vanlandingham, Instructor of Percussion, Baylor University
Bernard Roy Wexler, Sales Manager, David Wexler & Company
Robert Zildjian, Avedis Zildjian Company

The authors are particularly grateful for the extensive help of John Baldwin, Maurie Lishon, Al Payson, and Gordon Peters, who supplied many excellent suggestions for this book and spent countless hours in reading the manuscript.

The authors are also indebted to the following faculty members at Michigan State University for their advice and help: George Duerksen, Russell Friedewald, Paul Harder, Jere Hutcheson, Theodore Johnson, Loren Jones, Albert Laguire, James Niblock, Charles F. Schuller, Merrell Sherburn, Robert Sidnell, William R. Sur, and Arch Watson.

Acknowledgement is also due Gene Hemmle and Dean Killion of the Texas Technological College music department faculty, and to James Beckham, Norman Flanagan, Robert Mayes, and Gary Sherman for their assistance with photography.

Further, the many graduate composition students at Michigan State University and Texas Technological College deserve our gratitude for their suggestions and patience in testing some of the problems presented in this book.

Appendix 3:
Suppliers of
Percussion Instruments

MANUFACTURERS AND DEALERS

Amrawco, 8550 West 43rd Street, Lyons, Illinois 60534

C. Bruno & Sons, Inc., 3043 E. Commerce Street, San Antonio, Texas 78200

Camco Drum Company, 9221 South Kilpatrick Avenue, Oaklawn, Illinois 60453

Casa Veerkamp, S.A., Grandes Almacenes de Musica, 2a Mesones 21, Apartado 851, Mexico, D.F.

J.C. Deagan, Inc., 1770 West Berteau Avenue, Chicago, Illinois 60613

Drum City, 6226 Santa Monica Boulevard, Hollywood, California 90038

Evans Products, Inc., P.O. Box 58, Dodge City, Kansas 67801

Vic Firth, Symphony Hall, Boston, Massachusetts 02115

Saul Goodman, 141 Kneeland Avenue, Yonkers, New York 10700

Gon Bops of California, 970 Court Street, Los Angeles, California 90012

Fred Gretsch Manufacturing Company, 60 Broadway, Brooklyn, New York 10011

Fred Hinger, 206 Heritage Road, Cherry Hill, New Jersey 08034

M. Hohner, Inc., Andrews Road, Hicksville, L. I., New York 11800

G.C. Jenkins Company, P.O. Box 149, Decatur, Illinois 62525

Latin Percussion, 230 Parkway, Maywood, New Jersey 07607

Leedy Drum Company, 6633 N. Milwaukee Avenue, Niles, Illinois 60648

Ludwig Drum Company, 1728 North Damen Avenue, Chicago, Illinois 60647

Musser-Kitching, Inc., 505 E. Shawmut, La Grange, Illinois 60525

M.M. Paiste & Sohn, K.G., 6207 Nottwil/Lucerne, Switzerland

Payson Percussion Products, 2130 Glanville Ave., Park Ridge, Illinois 60068

Premiere Drum, Inc., 825 Lafayette Street, New Orleans, Louisiana 70130

Remo, Inc., 12804 Raymer Street, North Hollywood, California 91605

Rogers Drums, 1005 East 2nd Street, Dayton, Ohio 45402

Slingerland Drum Company, 6633 N. Milwaukee Avenue, Niles, Illinois 60648

Valje Drums, 3314 Sunset Boulevard, Los Angeles, California 90026

Avedis Zildjian Company, 39 Fayette Street, North Quincy, Massachusetts 02171

Zimgar Products, Inc., 81 Prospect Street, Brooklyn, New York 11200

RENTAL SHOPS

Carroll Music Instrument Service, 209 West 48th Street, New York, New York 10036

Drum City, 6226 Santa Monica Blvd., Hollywood, California 90038

Franks Drum Shop, Inc., 226 S. Wabash Avenue, Chicago, Illinois 60604

Professional Drum Shop, 854 Vine Street, Hollywood, California 91638

West Coast Drum Shop, 414 N. Broadway, Santa Ana, California 92700

(Many instruments, not shown in percussion manufacturers' catalogs, can be purchased from rental shops.)

EDUCATIONAL RHYTHM INSTRUMENTS

C. Bruno & Sons, Inc., 3043 E. Commerce Street, San Antonio, Texas 78200

Children's Music Center, Inc., 5373 W. Pico Blvd., Los Angeles, California 90019

Conn Corporation, 1101 E. Beardsley Street, Elkhart, Indiana 46514

Educational Music Bureau, 434 S. Wabash Avenue, Chicago, Illinois 60605

M. Hohner, Inc., Andrews Road, Hicksville, Long Island, N.Y. 11800

G.C. Jenkins Company, P.O. Box 149, Decatur, Illinois 62525

B.F. Kitching & Company, 505 Shawmut Street, La Grange, Illinois 60525

Ludwig Drum Company, 1728 North Damen Avenue, Chicago, Illinois 60647

Lyon Band Instrument Company, 223 S. Wabash Avenue, Chicago, Illinois 60606

Lyon-Healy, 223 West Lake Street, Chicago, Illinois 60606

Pearson Gourd Farm, 1409 N. Merced Avenue, Box 310, El Monte, California 91731

Peripole, Inc., 51–17 Rockaway Beach Blvd., Far Rockaway, Long Island, New York 11691

Rhythm Band, Inc., 407–409 Throckmorton Street, Fort Worth, Texas 76101

Targ & Dinner, Inc., 2451 N. Sacramento Street, Chicago, Illinois 60605

David Wexler & Company, 823 S. Wabash Avenue, Chicago, Illinois 60605

Index

141